BEYOND THE
WONDER

T0272354

BEYOND THE WONDER

AN ECOLOGIST'S VIEW OF WILD ALASKA

THOMAS BANCROFT

WSU
PRESS

Washington State University Press
Pullman, Washington

Washington State University Press
PO Box 645910
Pullman, Washington 99164-5910
Phone: 800-354-7360
Email: wsupress@wsu.edu
Website: wsupress.wsu.edu

© 2024 by the Board of Regents of Washington State University
All rights reserved
First printing 2024

Printed and bound in the United States of America on pH neutral, acid-free paper. Reproduction or transmission of material contained in this publication in excess of that permitted by copyright law is prohibited without permission in writing from the publisher.

Library of Congress Cataloging-in-Publication Data

Names: Bancroft, Thomas, 1951- author.
Title: Beyond the wonder : an ecologist's view of wild Alaska / Thomas
    Bancroft.
Description: Pullman, Washington : Washington State University Press,
    [2024] | Includes bibliographical references and index.
Identifiers: LCCN 2024026605 | ISBN 9780874224313 (paperback) | ISBN
    9780874224351 (hardback)
Subjects: LCSH: Bancroft, Thomas, 1951---Travel. | Environmental
    monitoring--Alaska--Citizen participation. | Wilderness areas--Alaska. |
    Environmental sciences--Alaska. | Human ecology--Alaska. | BISAC:
    BIOGRAPHY & AUTOBIOGRAPHY / Environmentalists & Naturalists | TRAVEL /
    United States / West / Pacific (AK, CA, HI, OR, WA)
Classification: LCC GE155.A4 B36 2024 | DDC 557.98--dc23/eng/20240815
LC record available at https://lccn.loc.gov/2024026605

frontispiece |

The sockeye dashes through the shallows of Funnel Creek, trying desperately to out-maneuver the pursuing brown bear.

All images in this volume are copyrighted by Thomas Bancroft. These and additional photos can be found on www.thomasbancroft.com.

The Washington State University Pullman campus is located on the homelands of the Niimíipuu (Nez Perce) Tribe and the Palus people. We acknowledge their presence here since time immemorial and recognize their continuing connection to the land, to the water, and to their ancestors. WSU Press is committed to publishing works that foster a deeper understanding of the Pacific Northwest and the contributions of its Native peoples.

Cover design by Patrick Brommer | Interior design by Tracy Randall

DEDICATION

To
Ann, Kelsie, Connor, and Elara Jane—
my family.
May nature always bring you joy and solace.

CONTENTS

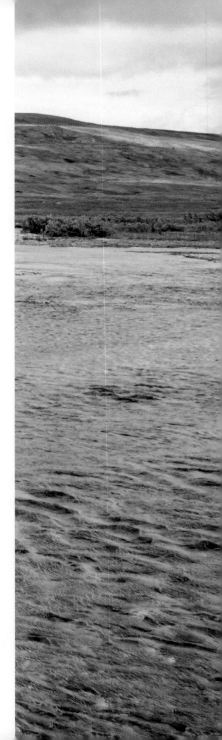

PREFACE

The Alaska brown bear *Ursus arctos* is an apex predator more popularly known as the grizzly. The image of this mammal often stimulates a strong feeling of awe and creates a sense of fear in humans. This bear symbolizes wildness at its loftiest—a place where the natural world can function unconstrained by humans. My professional career focused on understanding wild places and how to restore and protect them so native species could continue to survive and flourish. Seeing this bear was a dream.

Before I wrote this book, I had seen grizzlies a few times. The first, in 2003, was from the main road in Denali National Park. A large, probably male, grizzly was sleeping in the tundra a few hundred yards out. At the sight of this impressive bruin, I leapt toward that side of the bus for a better look, but it didn't twitch a muscle in the five minutes I watched it. In 2005, my wife Ann, daughter Kelsie, and I saw a female grizzly with two cubs running down the Kenai River. The bear family was way off, though, and we had only glimpses of them. A third time, in 2008, I was in a caravan of cars in Grand Teton National Park that stopped to watch a young grizzly run through the forest and disappear over a ridge. But I had never seen grizzlies just living their lives, being bears undisturbed by humans.

In 2018, my friend Bob Harvey posted photos on the Nature Photography Adventures website from a photography trip to the Katmai Peninsula in Alaska. His photographs were breathtaking. They showed bears fishing, wrestling, grazing, and just being themselves. Sockeyes ran the rivers, and the landscape was wild. I returned to his website many times over the next several months before finally contacting him about going on the next Katmai trip. It would be my chance to observe these magnificent creatures up close and experience their wildness.

When I arrived at the Katmai Peninsula in August 2019, I thought the trip was all about photography, but I soon discovered that the landscape and its creatures opened a floodgate of introspection. I had spent the first part of my professional career as a research scientist trying to understand birds and their habitats and what was needed to restore and protect them. Then, I moved into the science–policy interface, trying to translate science into forms that could influence laws, regulations, and management regimes. By the time of this trip, my salaried career had ended and I had begun to think about who I had been and who I was now.

We all have ups and downs, and I had just passed through a challenging decade during which Ann, my wife of thirty years, died of cancer, I also was diagnosed with cancer, I lost my job, and then I had to close a struggling organization, which forced me to sack its entire wonderful staff.

facing page |

A bear family comes to Moraine Creek to begin fishing. Sockeyes are an essential food for these bears, and they must put on a lot of fat for their hibernation.

On top of all that, my daughter—my only child—moved to another continent. Though I was still in the "healing phase," I realized that this week in Alaska might help me see the world beyond my grief and loss. Who had I become? Who might I become?

The bears, the landscape, and the wilds were mesmerizing, intricate, and complex. The trip consumed my mind and ignited my sense of wonder and possibility. I decided I would write a book as a lens into the experience, the place, and what it meant to me. The natural world provides many benefits, and being out in it has been a source of solace for me. I hope that the resulting combination of text and photographs will engender strong feelings in you, the reader—foremost, a sense of awe as you accompany me on this journey.

As our human population grows, a new and more comprehensive conservation strategy is needed. Critical to that effort will be having more people who care about wild places, whether or not they ever get to visit them. This book attempts to make sense of what I saw, thought, and—most importantly—felt in the midst of nature. I hope it will transport you to the same magical place and engender the same sense of wonder and possibility in you that I experienced, and leave you with much to ponder.

CHAPTER 1 | Port Alsworth Bay, Alaska

The sun was still half an hour from rising, and a heavy blue cast hung over the bay. In three hours, we were scheduled to head out by float-plane to look for brown bears, but I awoke early and couldn't get back to sleep. Clenching my arms tightly to my chest, I stared east along the mountains bordering Lake Clark, puzzled by my unsettled mood.

Katmai was powerfully wild country, home to all the creatures that had thrived here since long before Europeans came to North America. A few hundred people lived in tiny Port Alsworth, but the land was nearly free of humans for a hundred miles in all directions. A few Native villages south on Alaska's Katmai Peninsula had been here for millennia, but this vast country seemed entirely unaltered by contemporary humans.

Though I grew up on a Pennsylvania farm, I had lived and worked in cities my whole adult life and dedicated myself to protecting the wildest remaining parts of the natural world. Now, I had come to Alaska to truly immerse myself in that wildness in its most primeval form. With luck, I would get to see the untamed inhabitants of this untamed wilderness. Yet, here, on the brink of my adventure, sleep eluded me.

Clouds drifted across the rugged mountains at dawn. Pine siskins began to chatter in the conifers behind me, and the bawl of an unknown animal—a bear, a bird—sounded from across the water. Intense energy seemed to emanate from all directions. My eyes darted one way and then another, but I stood still, transfixed. This land was vibrant, alive, and untrammeled. Slowly, I could feel my mind and body connect with the quiet, deep rhythms of the true wild. In front of me was the thing I had searched for and strived to protect all my life. I was filled with reverence.

The rising sun began to peek through the clouds. I was ready.

facing page and detail right |

The sun is half an hour from rising, and a heavy blue cast hangs over the bay. I clench my arms tightly to my chest and stare east along the mountains bordering Lake Clark.

CHAPTER 2 | The Glance of the Grizzly

His eyes glared and his muscles tensed as he stood in two feet of churning water. I shifted my tripod to the right for a clearer view. He bolted forward, instantly at full speed, and headed downstream toward me. My finger pressed the shutter button; images came as fast as the camera's shutter could click. He pushed a wall of water in front of him, and splashes went up over his head, drenching his brownish-blond hair. The guy kept coming, less than a hundred yards away, running full tilt, his lips parted, teeth showing. My right hand held the camera pressed tight onto my eye. My left hand rested on the top of the lens, steadied by the gimbal head of my tripod. I tried to keep this brown bear in the center of the camera's frame as he kept coming, filling more and more of the viewfinder while the shutter snapped.

Other cameras clicked around me. Eight of us were bunched together on the edge of Funnel Creek in Katmai National Park. It was late afternoon, and we still had more than a mile-long hike across the tundra to where our two floatplanes sat tied to the shore of Mirror Lake. This brown bear had stopped us. We first saw him sound asleep beside the trail, but now he was charging toward us. I was torn. This was scary and I felt my body tensing, but I wanted to capture this blitz. Perhaps, though, we should become defensive? The bear must have weighed at least five hundred pounds, and his eyes seemed glued to me. Had Glen Alsworth Jr. and Leo Fowler, our two pilot guides, pulled out their .45s?

Nicole's comment from twenty years ago popped briefly into my mind. Her safety guidance on brown bears had given me the heebie-jeebies. As the new vice president of The Wilderness Society's Research Department, one of my responsibilities was to help bring a science component to our work in this state. I had flown to Alaska from Washington, DC, to spend several days with the regional staff of The Wilderness Society. After a few days in Anchorage, Allen Smith, Nicole Whittington-Evans, Darrell Knuffke, and I had left for a weekend canoe trip into the Kenai National Wildlife Refuge. This trip was a chance for us to discuss issues in one of the places we were working to protect.

Our canoes were ready to launch when Nicole tapped my arm. "We need to chat about bears," she said. "Stay together on portages, always talk out loud, even if you're alone, and don't run if you come across a grizzly; they will usually back down." Each of us had to make three trips across a mile-long portage, and we became separated while concentrating on the task. I stopped dead in my tracks in the middle of a dense spruce forest when I realized I was by myself. I had not been talking to the forest, but I did from then on.

Two decades later, here I stood in grizzly territory, with a prime specimen rushing right toward me, his eyes glaring. A bright red sockeye suddenly shot up in front of him, splashing water as its tail whipped back and forth. The bear couldn't resist it.

facing page |

The brown bear bolts forward, instantly at full speed, coming directly toward us. His glare cuts right through my telephoto lens, causing me to blink.

The salmon darted to our right, with the bear in full pursuit, and then headed away from us upstream.

I stepped back from my tripod. All eight of us were still there. Glen Jr. stood eight feet to my right and slightly closer to the bear. As the owner-manager of Farm Lodge in Port Alsworth, he was there to guide and protect us. His muscles were relaxed, his face calm with no visible sweat.

My arms were still tense.

Glen's shoulders were broad and his stance confident. His reddish beard glistened in the afternoon light. Katmai was his country. His grandfather, Babe Alsworth, had homesteaded the area along Lake Clark, which is now named after him. His father, Glen Sr., who runs Lake Clark Air, had flown us from Anchorage to Port Alsworth the previous day.

facing page |

A salmon darts in front of the charging bear. The flick of the sockeye's caudal fin creates a massive splash. The bear can't resist and pivots to follow.

The red sockeye bolts right in a desperate attempt to outmaneuver the brown bear, but this young male is as quick as a cutting horse and makes the turn to follow.

The young male brown bear pauses after lunging and missing a sockeye, looking right across Funnel Creek to where we stand. Perhaps he is considering an alternative meal.

Glen announced, "He's a young male, four or five years old, not fully mature," as if that explained everything. Glen chatted with all of us as if we were in a coffee shop in Anchorage and not out in wild Alaska where a brown bear had just run full speed right toward us. I shivered, each hand tightly gripping the bicep on the other arm as I wondered how Glen could be so calm. These bears are major predators, easily capable of taking down a moose or a caribou. A swipe from one of those forepaws would tear me to shreds. I shifted my feet around as another shiver ran through my body, and then I looked out at the creek. That charge had been thrilling. Though it scared me, somehow I didn't freeze or bolt but stayed focused on picture-taking. Right then, I was more awake than seemed possible. Watching this massive predator come charging at us made me wonder what had driven me to go on this trip. I had thought it was to photograph bears, but my mood this morning had made me begin to ponder—and now this.

The bear stood where the river tumbled over small rapids, looking back and forth in one direction and the next. Salmon were clearly in his sight, but he shook his thick coat and scowled in our direction. He seemed unsure about whether to eat salmon or us. Water dripped from his muzzle and muscular flanks. The Alaska Peninsula brown bear is a subspecies of *Ursus arctos*. Most people recognize it as the grizzly bear—the inland version—but such bears don't grow as big as these salmon-eating giants. Even more massive are the brown bears that live on Kodiak Island, where the incredible riches of the ocean help them grow to gigantic proportions.

Before flying out in search of bears earlier that day, we had huddled around the two floatplanes. Mark Kolka, Dan Davis, and I were assigned to Glen's plane, and the others—Joanne Rowan, Jay Robins, and Bob Harvey—were assigned to Leo's. A relay formed, and we handed our bags and tripods from person to person to be packed in the back of the planes. When Mark took my bright yellow dry bag, the weight caused it to sag a foot. "Yikes! You're going to carry all these?" he asked. "They seem to weigh forty pounds!" That bag didn't include my two tripods. Bob had said that the hike to Moraine Creek was not far, so I had brought everything.

Dan climbed nimbly into the front seat and slid across to the right side. I climbed in next, shuffling along the pontoon. A crossbar formed a giant first step, leaving a second step of equal distance into the cockpit. My waders clung tightly to my legs, but my feet slipped around inside the boots. Once in the plane, I leaned over and used my weight to move awkwardly into the back, where I slid over to the far side, feeling that Grace and Elegance had deserted me that morning. Mark climbed in beside me with ease, his camera in tow.

Glen stood on the top step and leaned over his seat. "Fasten your seatbelts. No smoking. There's an emergency beacon in the tail, and you can activate it with that red button." He pointed to the dash and a toggle switch. "There's a GPS locator signal on the yellow device on the top, and there's a fire extinguisher on the floor by the

copilot's seat. The orange bag behind you," he said as he pointed at Dan and me, "has two headsets for you." With that, he climbed in, buckled up, and moved confidently about his tasks. I guessed he was in his forties. He'd probably flown customers like us thousands of times.

I cinched up my seatbelt. It was my first time on a floatplane. I had spent several hundred hours in Cessna 172s and 182s when I worked in Florida, always fighting seasickness. My stomach was already queasy. "Keep your head vertical, and watch the horizon," I told myself in my mind, remembering the advice of John Ogden—my boss in Florida—when I was studying wading birds there. I wanted to photograph this country and see it the way a bird might. How could I have forgotten my Dramamine?

Glen cranked the engine and taxied out into the bay. The other Cessna began to plow water in huge waves off the fronts of both pontoons, and a giant wake formed behind it. The plane initially leaned up at a steep angle as it accelerated. It then rose onto the surface, lifted off the water and climbed rapidly, banking left out over Lake Clark.

Now it was our turn. Glen began to rev the propeller, and the plane lurched forward. The water's resistance held it back as the engine strained to speed us along. It took maybe a thousand feet before the back end suddenly lifted and the strain lessened noticeably. We bounced over small ripples on the bay for another thousand feet. Waves flew out from the pontoons, and then we lifted, gaining altitude, following Leo southwest. Camera in hand, I continued taking pictures throughout the takeoff, zooming the lens in and out for different perspectives.

The plane climbed, turning south, away from the lake. My forehead was pressed tight against the window. Spruce forests extended across the rolling hills. There were clumps of brown, dead trees interspersed among the living ones. Spruce beetles had reached the Katmai Peninsula. I used my finger to trace a small stream meandering through the forest, stopping on a beaver pond and the dam the rodents had built. Shortly, the spruce gave way to tundra, and I leaned back, staring forward, holding my head still and letting my stomach calm down.

As Glen weaved our plane through a narrow valley, my camera banged on my face and the window with each bounce of turbulence. Partway up the slope, the tundra disappeared, and the hillside became bare dirt spotted with dark, lichen-looking patches. Possibly caribou food? The hilltop wasn't visible because of the wing and fog.

"What's this pass called?" I asked Glen.

"It doesn't really have a name, he said. "We just call it High Notch."

The words "High Notch" went back and forth through my mind. We were passing over wild country, and its extent was hard to comprehend. Shortly, we would leave Lake Clark National Park,

facing page |

Spruce forests line the streams, and tundra covers the rolling hills south of Lake Clark. Spruce budworms have arrived in this region, killing many spruce trees. Warming temperatures have allowed the beetle to gain a foothold in Alaska and are changing its forest dynamics.

an area of four million acres, and fly across vast stretches of state and Alaska Native corporation lands that were equally wild and large, and then into Katmai National Park and Preserve, which was bigger than the states of Connecticut and Rhode Island combined. Helping The Wilderness Society build its program in Alaska had been especially rewarding because all the ecosystems' pieces were still there. Aldo Leopold, a great naturalist and writer and one of the founders of The Wilderness Society, said that it was essential to keep all the parts of the wheel if you wanted it to work. In Alaska, we could.

Forty minutes later, we began to descend toward two lakes in the center of a broad valley. Twice more, I had to stop looking down and taking pictures to instead watch the horizon until my stomach settled. I had seen trails meandering through the tundra (maybe made by caribou), lines in the lake vegetation (maybe from a moose), beaver dams, trumpeter swans, and numerous rivers running wild, unimpeded by human devices. Western culture is all about control, exploitation, conquering the wilderness, but this land hadn't suffered from these assaults.

Glen got my attention when he called Leo over the radio and said that he would make a loop from Mirror Lake down along Funnel Creek to see what was there. He cruised about four hundred feet above the ground. The creek was visible from his side of the plane. I craned my neck to look out the opposite window. I could make out at least two large brown figures standing in the water. My muscles tightened. I couldn't wait to get out of the plane and walk into their world.

Throughout my life, the wilds have been a source of awe for me. I've often stood and marveled at what I saw, contemplating the existence, evolution, or geologic reason for what was there. One of my earliest memories as a child was of my sister Barbie asking if I wanted to "go to the wilderness" on our family's farm. She took me below the barn, where we crawled through a long tunnel formed by overhanging hog wire and brambles, coming out into a meadow among the walnut trees. It was simultaneously thrilling and scary. Only four years old at the time, I would have promised my seven-year-old sister anything to ensure that she would get me back home safely.

When my life fell apart six years ago, I sought solace in Washington's wilderness areas. The downhill spiral started in 2004 when Ann was diagnosed with ovarian cancer at age fifty-two; her prognosis was never good. For thirty months, she fought the disease, taking chemotherapy in one form or another virtually the entire time. She desperately hoped to see Kelsie graduate from college, marry, and have a child; and she never wanted to talk about her illness or pending death. While caring for her and grappling with the pressures of my work—leading a department at The Wilderness Society—I never fully faced that reality either.

Ann slipped into a coma one day in December 2006 and died a week later. It was Kelsie's senior year in college. In September 2007, I foolishly changed jobs, probably to escape my grief. The position of chief scientist at National Audubon seemed like a great opportunity to get back to studying birds. A month later, though, I was diagnosed with prostate cancer and slipped into depression.

As I endeavored to climb out of my gloom, a new organizational leader at Audubon decided to fire most of the existing senior staff, including me. I made the mistake of taking the first job offer I received, despite having to move clear across the country, even though I had a feeling something wasn't right about it. Off I went to Seattle to lead a small nonprofit that focused on Puget Sound conservation.

The distance strained my relationship with my daughter. To make matters worse, I discovered that my new Seattle employer was experiencing severe financial problems. These had not been revealed to me during my interview, and yet they were now my responsibility to solve. After spending two years trying to save the organization, the board and I decided to close its doors. The ordeal exhausted me, mind and body. During the year that followed, I solo-backpacked into more than twenty of Washington's designated wilderness areas, often in places so remote that I saw few people for days on end, which suited me entirely.

Glen banked the plane around, snapping my thoughts back from the past. "This looks good to me. I saw four or five bears. Let's stop here." Both

planes flew upstream to the far end of Mirror Lake, landing and taxiing to the north shore, a good half mile from the lake's end and the creek where Glen had spotted the bears. He cut the engine and adjusted the rudders so we turned to face the wind and drifted back toward shore.

"Stay here," Glen told Mark, Dan, and me as he jumped onto the pontoon and into the lake, the water almost coming to his knees. After dragging the plane until both floats were sitting against the shore, he came back for us. We unloaded the camera equipment with a relay team and prepared it for the day. I had come equipped with two cameras, a pair of binoculars around my neck, a heavy backpack, two tripods, and my chest waders pulled high—fifty-plus pounds in all.

I shifted the weight around my body while slipping in the loose gravel. When I caught my balance, I noticed Bob Harvey staring at me. "You want another tripod?" he asked with a chuckle, but I could see the concern on his face. He was a little younger than me, with silver hair. He carried his camera gear easily, not visibly strained by its substantial weight. Everyone had brought big lenses. Bob had organized this trip, and it was through his company, Nature Photography Adventures, that I'd signed up. Moraine Creek, where I thought we were headed, was a short walk, but Funnel Creek would require a few miles' journey to our photography locations.

The loose gravel on the berm proved challenging to traverse. Not only did my boots slip, but my feet inside my waders slid back and forth. A trail in the tundra made for a more comfortable walk. However, it wasn't long before we stepped over small piles of black scat filled with partially digested blueberries and dogwood berries. I suddenly realized that we were walking on a bear trail. It made me hesitate and look a second time at some scat. I was really here, on the tundra of Alaska, where giant brown bears roamed freely, and we were walking toward the place where they would be feeding. I quickened my steps, but it wasn't long before I started to lag behind the others. The weight of my gear was taking its toll.

The group dropped down a small berm to stand beside the outlet of Mirror Lake and the start of Funnel Creek. Everyone waded immediately across the flow except Bob, who stood with his right hand on his hip, and his head cocked slightly toward me. "You okay?" I nodded, but he looked concerned. The crystal-clear water flowed rapidly over a rocky bottom. Each stone was distinct through knee-deep water, and the current pushed hard against my calves. I leaned upstream, taking mini steps to keep my balance. Bob moved beside me, looking nonchalant, but he kept glancing my way every three or four feet. Glen waited on the far shore.

"Need a hand?" Glen asked as he reached out, extending his body over the bank's edge.

facing page |

After landing on Mirror Lake, we begin the hike to Funnel Creek. Winter winds have pushed ice drifts up onto the shoreline, forming the wide rocky beaches.

I grabbed his wrist, and he pulled me and all my gear up the bank. "Thanks," I said as we shuffled to follow the others. Glen tipped his head, averting his eyes while hurrying along. I relaxed, having successfully crossed seventy-five feet of rushing water. It scared me more than I expected. I had used my big tripod to steady myself while balancing the weight of all the camera equipment on my back. A slip with chest waders would have been disastrous, to put it mildly, especially if my waders filled with water and my cameras got soaked.

The creek ran for a third of a mile before opening into a small pond. About halfway along that stretch, someone pointed north. A little brown blob plodded across the tundra, probably a half mile away. Even through my ten-power telephoto lens, it looked small, but it was my first wild brown bear, and I stood on the tundra in its domain. The blond-backed guy passed in front of a large patch of pink fireweed. He was heading up into the hills, and I thought, "Oh, no," worried that this would be our only sighting. As the others continued toward the edge of the next pond, I stood photographing him. When I put down my camera, I saw that I was several hundred feet behind everyone else. Leo had stopped to wait for me, but I hurried to catch up, remembering a conversation from the previous night as well as my friend Nicole's long-ago warning about staying together in bear country.

On the preceding day, we had arrived late in the afternoon, settled into our cabins, and then headed to the lodge for dinner. The six of us had just finished eating and were chatting when Dan said, "I'm still really nervous about this trip." He looked away from everyone, paused, and added, "Those bears scare me." Dan was a tall man and didn't look his age. I suspected he was in his seventies or close to it. Yet, he walked with an appearance of youth and vigor. The way he talked made me wonder if he'd been a university professor.

The level of tension around the table skyrocketed. I felt my muscles tighten. Dan hesitated for a few seconds and then stared at Bob, saying, "I read about Timothy Treadwell and everything I could find on others who were killed by bears." Treadwell and his girlfriend had been killed and eaten by a brown bear on the Katmai Peninsula. Dan's hands gripped the table's edge as if he were about to bolt for the exit, and his face was taut. Everyone's face was frozen and expressionless, and we were all looking at Bob.

"Timothy was asking for it," said Bob as he sipped his lemonade. He glanced at each of us and then fixed his eyes on Dan as he set his glass back on the table. "Timothy and his girlfriend tried to live with the bears, camping along bear trails and the shore, even walking right among them as they fished for salmon." Bob straightened and became taller as he emphasized the mistakes

Treadwell had made. I marveled at his calmness and appreciated his effort to get us to relax.

An old male, not in good shape, had killed the two of them. I remember it making headlines because the deaths were captured in Werner Herzog's documentary *Grizzly Man*. I had intentionally not reviewed anything on bears killing humans before this trip and definitely had not watched Herzog's movie. Bob continued, "We will stay together and away from the bears. Our guides carry guns and really know the local bears. They haven't had any issues."

The tension around the dinner table remained high, but then someone, I think Mark, joked, "You need to learn how to use your tripod to trip one of us, just not me," and everyone laughed, releasing the tension. "Or just not be the slowest," I thought.

As I hurried to catch up with Leo along the edge of Funnel Creek, I knew the rest had marked me as the slowest. About a mile down the creek was a small waterfall with a five-foot drop. Salmon congregated below the falls and were sluggish after making it to the top. My ecological training told me that this would be a perfect place for a bear to fish. We slid down the embankment to a large rock outcrop fifty feet from the falls. We immediately saw a black-furred male standing right at the creek's edge. I could have tossed a baseball to him. He was alert, stiff, and tall as he stared across the one hundred feet of shallow water, ready to leap.

Up to this point, the idea of being close to bears in their domain had merely been theoretical. I knew about bears and salmon, but here were both of them, poised for a showdown. We discussed the concept of "wild" when I was at The Wilderness Society. Perhaps having a predator such as a bear, who could easily eat me, was a central part of that idea. Protecting landscapes such as this one was always our goal, and now I stood here with a massive predator who appeared hungry.

Camera shutters started clicking as the dark male moseyed across the creek. Salmon darted one way and another, but he just glanced at them. Apparently, when salmon are abundant, bears gorge themselves, eating several dozens a day. Then, they become highly picky, going only for easy fish, and may eat only the fatty skin and the roe. They're like the relative at Thanksgiving dinner who picks at the platters, taking special tidbits from here and there. When he reached the other side, the bear turned downstream and quickly disappeared around a bend.

We settled to wait for more action, our cameras, with their big lenses, secured to tripods and lunches emerging from packs. Several dozen bright red sockeyes congregated in the swift-moving water below the falls, another half dozen lazily lurked in an eddy right under our perch, and others could be seen in the shallows above and below the falls. These were looking for suitable spawning places. Salmon were abundant, but my thoughts were still on bears.

The dark one was massive, probably at least eight hundred pounds, his muscles taut, his head enormous—bigger than a basketball—and his claws long and curved, the size of my little finger.

facing page |

A massive adult male brown bear steps onto a rock in Funnel Creek. He is only the distance between first base and home plate—ninety feet— and he never acknowledges our presence.

The claws on this bear are as big as my fingers, and his feet are far larger than both of mine put together.

Strength seemed to radiate from him, his sharp eyes were intense even at a distance, and he held his head proudly. His color was darker than I expected, almost black, with a few light-brown hairs around his ears. Someone pointed to another bear sleeping on the bank just downstream. It was as big as a large chest freezer.

I looked up and down at my overweight body—with a body mass index of twenty-seven, the heaviest I'd been in sixty-seven years—and then out across the water. I would be a tender morsel in such a bear's quest to reach hibernation condition. I felt tiny right then, insignificant in the scheme of things. Our perch was down in a ravine; only upstream could we see beyond the high banks. There, tundra stretched for miles before mini mountains with large snow patches rose on the landscape. We had flown over two small villages on Iliamna Lake; otherwise, we had seen no evidence of human habitation in the ninety-mile flight from Port Alsworth. Imagine no one living between Seattle and the Canadian border or between Baltimore and Philadelphia.

facing page |

A blond rug lies on the tundra at the edge of Funnel Creek. A dozen or more sockeyes lurk in the water just below the nose of this sleeping bear.

Funnel Creek weaves through the valley from Mirror Lake. Tundra covers the valley bottom, switching to lichen as its slopes climb into the foothills.

A bear stands on a rock to survey the sockeyes swimming upstream in Funnel Creek. Fireweed dots the slope behind him.

This country was untrammeled by humans. Here, nature could flow as it wished, influenced by weather, species interactions, and chance. I had spent my career trying to save wildlife, restore natural habitats, and protect species, but I had never actually been in a place that remained unaltered by humans in some fundamental way. A dozen salmon circled the pool below the falls, each approaching two feet long—bright red, and ready to breed. They needed to use their own strength and skill to make it up the falls and continue on their journey. Perhaps that's what this trip was all about: finding a country where humans were insignificant and unimportant in the annual cycle.

"Bear!" Glen called out, and I jumped. Above the falls, a blond individual was working its way along the bank. It walked through the willows and tundra more like a person on a stroll than someone bent on reaching a destination. My eye went to my camera, and the shutter started clicking. The bear came through a small opening, stepping out into the water, which appeared knee-deep.

Glen said, "This is the bear we saw walking across the tundra on the way down." I hadn't figured that out, and I admired Glen's awareness.

The animal became rigid, muscles tight, looking like a cat ready to pounce. Then he shot forward like a sprinter leaving the starting blocks, racing upstream thirty yards before doing a complete pirouette on his haunches and running full speed,

right toward us. My camera was snapping photographs at three frames a second, and I wished I had set it higher. He ran like a soccer professional going through a crowded defense. He curled left of one rock, then between two others, and around a third. All the time, his eyes seemed glued to something just in front of his feet. Then there was a lunge, and his head went into the water, creating a splash like someone doing a cannonball into a swimming pool.

The bear has been chasing this sockeye salmon for more than ten seconds and shows no sign of giving up. The bruin lunges for the sockeye and misses it, but he continues the pursuit.

The water completely covered his upper body. When his head rose from the creek, a bright red sockeye wiggled in his mouth, its tail whipping back and forth. The bear's left front foot was cupped over the front of his muzzle, much as my hand shoved the final piece of a sandwich into my mouth. He held still for several seconds, water dripping from his head in a thick stream, and then began to walk toward the far bank, teeth firmly gripping his prey, which continued to wiggle.

Later that night, I looked at the sequence of photographs, forty-two of them from start to capture, taken in fourteen seconds—the time it takes a world-class sprinter to run a hundred meters. This bear was doing that run through knee-deep water. Some photographs showed the redfish racing in front of the bear and the intensity of the bear's eyes

The sockeye dashes through the shallows of Funnel Creek, trying desperately to outmaneuver the pursuing brown bear.

The bear lunges forward, briefly pinning the sockeye with a giant paw, and then grabs the fish in its teeth, holding it with the back of his paw.

fixated on its quarry. They revealed the power of the bear's charge. His muscles were straining, his front feet extending out in giant leaps and swift turns. The salmon made a final dart at right angles to the bear and came a little out of the water. I could see its eyes and head. At that point, the bear lunged, pinning the fish to the bottom with his front paws and their long, dark claws. Then his head lunged in for the kill. I went back and forth over the photographs a dozen times, studying the bear in pursuit and watching the salmon. Each time, I noticed new details of both creatures' athleticism and grace, and the finesse of their movements. This episode heralded wildness—nature unimpeded by humans.

I couldn't get the image of that hunt out of my mind. The intensity of the bear's pursuit was like the power of an entire National Football League team packaged into one body as they exploded into a play. Then, the effort made by the salmon to escape was exceptional. The force of each twitch of that caudal fin shot the salmon like a bullet out of a muzzle. What had that salmon escaped over the last three or four years, only to be eaten now, before it reached its natal gravel bed? It made me think about my own prowess or lack thereof. Each year, I committed to getting into better shape. I had been walking the stairs near my house all this summer—all one hundred ninety-six of them. I do them two at a time, three times up, and then several more loops one at a time, working my leg muscles—not enough, though, to now comfortably carry all this camera gear.

A little after two o'clock, Glen said, "We need to start back as it will take a while. We might see something on the way." As I hefted the backpack onto my shoulders, my equipment seemed heavier than it had that morning. Leo had to help me up the hill to the tundra. He had broad shoulders that radiated strength, and I hadn't seen him even breathe hard on our hike this morning. He took my big tripod, set it behind him, and grabbed my hand, hefting me up. I probably felt like a sack of potatoes to him. He didn't say a word when I thanked him. I trudged after them, not wanting to admit that this was harder than I had expected and resolved to leave all the sound equipment and extra lenses behind the next day.

The plodding worsened; I told myself to concentrate on one foot at a time. I would alternate between holding a camera with one hand and using it to raise my backpack off my shoulders, letting the camera dangle from my sore neck. The other hand carried the big tripod, sometimes balancing it on my shoulders. The group had spread out over a hundred yards or more, but Leo always kept an eye on me, keeping me from falling too far behind. He must have looked back twenty or more times in the first mile. Everyone stopped abruptly, and as I caught up, I heard Glen say, "We will wait a while and see what he does. If we have to, we will go up around him." I looked around to see what he was talking about, not wanting to show my ignorance from being the lagger. There, sleeping only a few hundred feet in front of us, not far off the trail we'd hoped to walk, was the young blond male bear that had put on the chase for us down by the falls.

The bear awoke before long and did the mock charge I described at the beginning of this chapter. Might this male have come all the way to us if that salmon hadn't darted in front of him? Might he have made Glen and Leo react? Bears are well-known for charging and then breaking off before contact. It was thrilling to be here, especially now that the bear was focused on fishing.

facing page |

The brown bear runs full tilt in pursuit of a sockeye. The bear's eyes seem glued to the fish; his body responds instantly to each turn of the salmon.

The blond one raced back and forth in the stream, hunting salmon. He was a grand specimen—strong, robust, and putting on weight. In another few years, if he survived, he could become one of the dominant males in this sector of Katmai. Perhaps I could come back then and see him again. I watched him run; he was much like a cutting horse responding instantly to the twists and turns of a steer. This bear was the epitome of an athlete—everything I wished I could be.

I still have dreams of being an athlete—a high school football star like my brother Wilder, a basketball player like my sister Barbie, or maybe a baseball player. It never happened, never would, never could, no matter how much I wished it. I lacked the strength, endurance, and hand–eye coordination needed to be an athlete. My gym teachers in high school used to mock me when I couldn't do any chin-ups or as many push-ups as my schoolmates. I've often wondered if my severe asthma and bad allergies stunted my muscle development. Now, my desire to go deep into the wilderness while carrying camera and sound equipment or undertake long backpack hikes makes me envious of this bear's prowess.

Glen interrupted my thoughts. "We had better get going; still a way to walk." Another hour passed while we watched salmon and this bear.

"We need to give him a wide berth. Let's go up the hill and loop around him," Glen continued

Our group treks along the creek, returning to Mirror Lake and our floatplanes. We walk on bear trails.

as he walked up the gentle grade into the tundra almost perpendicular to the creek and then turned toward Mirror Lake.

We crossed Funnel Creek right at the out-flow from the lake. Again, I used my tripod to steady myself as I inched across the expanse of swift-moving water. Bob and Leo both stood by to rescue me if I faltered. I felt like a mollycoddle and promised myself to work on my weight and strength.

The lake's shoreline curved around toward where the two floatplanes rested. Our group spread out along the shore and the bear trail through the tundra, each of us walking alone, absorbed in thought. We had spent six hours here, embedded in the world of the Alaska Peninsula brown bear. We were in his domain, not ours. Four bears had blessed us with their time, yet I saw no indication that we had disturbed them.

I glanced at Bob, who was walking close to me, and wondered what he thought of these bears and their abilities. He was still monitoring my progress. I felt self-conscious about not having prepared for this trip as well as I thought. I didn't want to be taken care of in this way. I had dreamed about this country, and now I was here. It occurred to me, though, that my role in life had been to mollycoddle the environment and protect it as best as I could. Injecting science into policy and management had been the strategy, going beyond just creating new knowledge. Though I went to graduate school to become a university professor—someone whose job was to develop new knowledge—and my master's and dissertation topics were esoteric, I had not taken the opportunity to go the professor route when it was offered to me. Instead, I had jumped at the chance to sit in an office in Washington, DC, and focus on protecting wildlands like this.

facing page |

The skin on sockeye is rich in fats and nutrients. Bears pull long strips off to eat before moving to the flesh.

CHAPTER 3 | Still Adapting

The gulls formed a ring in the water, like a giant Hula-Hoop, maybe twelve feet in diameter. They all had white heads and were focused on the circle's center, where a large brown bear was tearing at his catch. Water came to the bear's shoulders, and he held the sockeye with both paws at water level. His teeth bit down on a chunk of skin, and then he extended his front legs as far as possible, pulling off the fatty flesh. His nose twisted up as he yanked, and his large cream-colored teeth occasionally showed. He sucked in the morsel like a long piece of spaghetti and then began with another. Meanwhile, the gulls appeared to be waiting for scraps to float out or for the carcass to be abandoned.

I had seen only adult glaucous-winged gulls in our three days on the Katmai Peninsula. Most of the time, they had been lurk-ing, waiting for action, much like me. Young gulls take three to four years to reach adult plumage, and I couldn't think why those adolescents hadn't found this food source. Our guides had taken us down Moraine Creek to search for bears that day. We had been to Funnel Creek and Brooks River on the previous two days. I'd expected lots of gulls, not just adults.

facing page |

The brown bear spots us as it approaches the creek. We were probably standing where it wanted to be, and it initially looked surprised before mosing to the water just beyond us.

Over a dozen glaucous-winged gulls circle a brown bear as it feeds on a sockeye. These birds move up Alaska's rivers when the salmon run.

"You're looking at seagulls again," snarked Mark. "How can you waste your time on those things?" When I looked his way, he had a smile on his face. He had been teasing me about gulls for three days now. During a lull in bear action on our first day, I was trying to capture a good flight shot of gulls as they flew up and down Funnel Creek. Their long wings, gray backs, white heads, and red-spotted yellow bills created a fascinating contrast to the creek's green-brown tundra and duller colors. Their flight was elegant, employing any breeze to fly effortlessly, holding their wings still, and if these birds needed to move quickly or get somewhere fast, a few flaps of their five-foot wingspan would shoot them through the air.

Glaucous-winged gulls breed along the Pacific coast from Washington north through Alaska, across the Bering Strait, and down the coast of Siberia to northern Japan. This species and its nineteen close relatives all have white heads as adults, are relatively large, and can be spotted along the shores of the Northern and Southern Hemispheres. They vary in the grayness of their backs and in how black their wingtips are. They wander outside the breeding range, and because they all look very similar, birders, including me, often complain about identifying gulls. However, one must admit that this "bird model" works well and that evolution has allowed gulls to adapt to local conditions worldwide.

Back on that first day, in response to Mark's comment, I had said, "There's no such thing as a 'seagull.' Besides, these glaucous-winged gulls stay primarily along the coast and go only a short way offshore." My major professor in graduate school would go ballistic if someone called a bird a seagull. Maybe you could call the two kittiwake species or Sabine's gulls seagulls since they're actually seagoing, but these others are either coastal or inland dwellers. Besides, I thought, calling them seagulls deprived them of dignity and recognition that they are unique, different, and adapted to where they lived.

Mark said his wife would be furious if he wasted time photographing seagulls. "They sit on our driveway in Wisconsin and crap all over it. We both hate them," he explained. He didn't seem impressed when I said he probably had ring-billed gulls there—definitely not this particular species. Ring-bills are much smaller and don't belong to the same group of gulls as the glaucous-winged. He barked, "How many pictures did you just take, a hundred?" I ran my motor drive and followed several individuals as they flew by, snapping away on each. Mark was a big man with broad shoulders. He talked forcibly about his feelings but also showed a level of respect for nature. He was fun to be around and often surprised me with his comments and humor.

I had not risen to Mark's tease three days after that first discussion. I simply responded, "Yeah, they sure are beautiful athletes, worth every chance to capture a great photograph." I went back to thinking about adaptability. The species is considered part of the "herring gull complex," a group of twenty gull species found worldwide. Each species has evolved to adapt to different conditions, and now at least one of these species inhabits the coastline of every continent. In graduate school, we had many discussions and arguments about how all these individual species could have evolved when their ranges overlapped. Evolutionary biologists thought that geographic isolation was required for speciation to happen. Currently, adjacent species often hybridize in their bands of overlap. With the advent of DNA analysis, ornithologists think there was probably isolation that allowed the initial evolution to happen. This made me wonder about my own adaptability.

Glaucous-winged gulls wait for a bear to finish its sockeye meal and, hopefully, leave them scraps.

Perhaps our mindset also adapts to changes, opportunities, and challenges. Although this is not a genetic change, it seems like a shift that helps us survive. I had moved cities eight times since high school, worked for six employers—seven if you include me—since graduate school, and even shifted careers more than once. Perhaps even now, at age sixty-seven, I was in that evolutionary process again.

The bear at the center of the circle of gulls dropped a chunk of fish meat, which floated out. Instantly, four of the gulls lunged for the morsel, and a tussle took place not a human body's length from the bear. One gull finally got control of the morsel and flew off, with two others in pursuit. This bird species is adapted to the Pacific Northwest. It interbreeds with the western gull along the coast of Washington. Ornithologists think that hybrids have some survival advantage in that zone but are selected against farther north and south. The hybridization region has expanded slightly in recent decades, but scientists don't think these two species will meld into one.

A glaucous-winged gull grabs a scrap of skin and flees the other gulls who continue to bicker over morsels.

That melding may be what's happening with the northern flicker. Back when I was in high school, this species was separated into yellow-shafted in eastern North America and red-shafted in the West. They interbreed, though, and the intergrade area seems to be expanding. Ornithologists have already lumped them into one species. Near my home in Seattle, I can sometimes find individuals with characteristics from both varieties.

Each time Ann, Kelsie, and I moved to a different city, we had to adapt to the new surroundings, develop new friendships, and learn to survive in new conditions and social environments. Developing new friends was always difficult alongside work and family responsibilities. Ann seemed much better than I at making friends quickly and adjusting to changes.

A few more gulls flew to the feeding bear, increasing the horde of bystanders. Annually, these gulls move in response to feeding opportunities. These were probably post-breeding adults who followed the salmon as they migrated up the rivers to spawn. After the salmon spawn, the gulls return to the coast and probably drift south as fall and winter approach. Next spring, they will come home to their breeding islands and start the process all over again. I had to look away for a second as I thought about my own peregrinations.

Since high school, I had wanted to be a research scientist and study birds. After finishing my PhD, I did that for a decade and then entered the policy arena. I left that job to return to a more academic post, but one that still had a conservation focus. The big switch occurred when I went off to DC for the science–policy interface. At that time, I was offered two jobs: one at a university, exactly the job I had dreamed of, and the other in DC, where I was to lead a research department that needed to be integrated into the conservation group's policy and management work.

When I couldn't decide which job to take, I called a friend I had worked with on Everglades issues. He paused, not wanting to steer me too much, then asked, "Can you do the job at the university?"

"Yes," I responded. "It's what I've been training for since high school."

"Can you do the job for The Wilderness Society?" he asked.

This time, I paused for a long while. "I don't know," I said.

The phone stayed silent, neither of us knowing what to say next. Finally, he spoke: "Well, knowing you, my guess is you would find the university job exciting, just what you wanted,"—long pause—"for maybe two or three years, and then you'd begin to wonder if you could have conquered that other challenge."

The brown bear walks away from its catch, and the gulls immediately move in to consume the scraps.

I took the DC job at The Wilderness Society and flew up for an all-staff planning meeting two months before starting. It scared the daylights out of me. I had been a wetland biologist specializing in birds and focusing on endangered species. Now I was to lead a department in an organization that didn't work on any of those things.

I had three charges. The first was to integrate the work of the Research Department into the policy and advocacy programs. The second was to help build a program with strong scientific credibility focused on lands overseen by the federal Bureau of Land Management. The Wilderness Society had a long history of working on national forest issues and influencing US Forest Service policy by using ecological, economic, and legal knowledge. We wanted something similar for the Bureau of Land Management. My third charge was to bring a science component to The Wilderness Society's Alaska agenda.

I left that meeting and spent five sleepless nights on a bicycle ride through Virginia with my brother-in-law. That job move, though, was one of the best decisions of my life. I almost failed at it several times, but in the end I evolved and adapted to meet the challenge. Bringing a strong science component to Alaska took a long time, but science–policy integration is still happening twelve years later.

The bear dropped the carcass of the sockeye and turned to mosey through the water. The gulls went into a frenzy, cawing, flapping, and tussling until all the scraps were consumed.

"Let's move down the creek some more and see what we can find," suggested Glen. We came to a broad, gentle, flowing section a quarter mile from where we had set off. There we found four bears spread across an area the size of several football fields. Two large males lay by themselves, napping on the short vegetation, and two smaller individuals sat not far from each other on a patch of sedges.

Someone asked about the two that seemed to be together. Glen said, "They're probably brothers. Often, they stay together for another year or two after their mother chases them out. I guess it's companionship." At least one hundred gulls loitered near the four bears, standing around, waiting for the bears to go back to feeding and give them something to do—in some ways, waiting for their lives to get going.

Glaucous-winged gulls wait for the resting bear to return to the water and fish. These birds follow the salmon up the rivers of Katmai National Park.

That waiting reminded me of how I felt after moving to Seattle, only to find that my job and the rest of my life there wasn't going as planned. The move took place a few years after Ann's death—Seattle was supposed to be a fresh start. Instead, I fell into a state of despair after losing my job, and it seemed I was in limbo, waiting for a reboot, just like all those gulls.

Our human identities are often defined by family and job, and I had neither. My daughter had moved to Australia, and my siblings lived on the East Coast. I had been a research scientist or conservationist throughout my professional life, and I found myself without the energy or motivation to take on another leadership role. Like those gulls, I was waiting; but, unlike me, maybe the gulls knew exactly what they were meant to do.

Why had Mark's seagull comment riled me so much? Over the previous four years, I had spent time leading field trips, teaching classes, giving presentations, and writing about nature. Naming living things correctly and pondering their lives and interactions had been central to that effort. As Robin Wall Kimmerer nicely articulates, by naming things, one recognizes them as different or unique and gives them a status they might not otherwise have. Maybe hearing Mark lumping the gulls into a bucket of "seagulls" was too much. Maybe I should have just started calling him "Wisconsin." That exchange with Mark reminded me why naming things is important.

In my teaching, I frequently helped people see the characteristics that highlight groups of birds, flowers, or trees. Encouraging people to practice identification in increments helped them avoid being overwhelmed. The first step was to learn that a thing was a gull, sparrow, warbler, pine, lupine, or daisy, and then to look for the finer details that allow species identification. So why the concern over "seagull"? Maybe my subconscious was saying that it was a slur—possibly unintentional but still derogatory—of a living organism. The name "seagull" could imply a lack of respect, a failure to acknowledge individuality or value.

However, the concepts of naming and adaptability seem almost like enigmas. In a lifetime sense, all individuals must adjust to the changing conditions they face, but on an evolutionary scale, a species must change as the conditions on earth change. So, does a single name imply something static, suspended in adaptation? I watched two gulls fly low along the river, as if they had an appointment upstream.

To the chagrin of birders, the American Ornithological Society makes a few adjustments to the taxonomy of birds in North America each year. These changes reflect the current scientific knowledge of species and relationships. Recently, the ornithologists had lumped Thayer's gull with the Iceland gull, two members of the same gull complex, because they're no longer thought to be separate species. However, a decade ago, taxonomists separated the yellow-footed gull from the western gull. Our naming also adapts.

The two big male bruins stretched and began to drift toward the water. As one approached the other, they raised their hackles, arched their backs, and threatened each other. They were in a mock display of pride and dominance. It was as if one was the research scientist in me and the other was that person focusing on policy. Perhaps I was still questioning the choice I had made two decades ago. Recently, I'd been worried about all the research projects I hadn't written and probably never would. Had I let science down?

At the end of our day on the river, the two younger bears began to stir, and the gulls responded by flying in circles around them. They strolled diagonally toward the creek, heading farther downstream from where we sat. Some gulls flew ahead while others lurked behind. The bears were now energized and might soon begin to feed.

The word "adaptability" kept popping back up in my mind. These bears were tightly linked to salmon runs for the added nutrients they needed to build their fat reserves for winter. The salmon

Two giant male brown bears threaten each other as they head back to the creek for some fishing.

had evolved, now using these freshwater creeks as places where their eggs and fry could develop and prosper, and the gulls had learned to exploit the opportunity, feeding on the scraps left by the bears and the spawned-out carcasses of salmon. It took me a couple of years, many solo backpack hikes into the wilderness, and a lot of therapy to climb out of my depression. Hope for my ability to continue adapting to what might come next grew in me. Maybe this trip was a chance to think about what's next for me: science, policy, or something else.

The two young males were still downstream, hunting salmon. Not exactly working together to fish, they were just enjoying life in proximity.

In another year or so, they would move apart, become independent, and probably greet each other with mock machismo. Might they be more like where I am now—alone, in some respects living in the moment while also harboring a desire for something more? I looked at Mark and the others—they were all photographing bears—and I suddenly realized that, in many respects, I am still evolving and adapting. Right now, I'm focusing on helping others experience the wild, name organisms, and see things they may not otherwise notice. This new direction may be okay.

One of the young brown bears began a vigorous chase of a redfish, and a glaucous-winged gull swooped along just a dozen feet behind.

facing page |

Two young brown bears, probably brothers, fish together along Moraine Creek. The glaucous-winged gulls lurk nearby, clearly hoping for leftovers.

CHAPTER 4 | Suk-kegh

I held my cell phone in my right hand, having set my binoculars, camera, and tripod on the tundra. The creek bank dropped only fifteen inches, but the water was crystal clear, and I couldn't tell how deep it was. I tugged on my waders, my feet slipping back and forth inside the boots, and wondered if I could do this without falling. My right foot went out over the creek, and the left quickly followed. The water reached my knees as I stumbled forward and found my footing.

My photography group milled around—a hundred feet back in the tundra. Glen, our guide, had made us pause on our hike back to the floatplanes because a five-hundred-pound brown bear was napping on the trail. It was midafternoon, and we had spent all day along Funnel Creek watching brown bears feed on sockeye salmon. The creek was full of fish, cruising here and there, swimming upstream. It was spawning time in Alaska's Katmai National Park and Preserve.

The waterproof cover I had brought for my phone would allow me to photograph salmon swimming. So, when Glen made us wait, I immediately asked if I could walk out into the creek. He glared at me for a few seconds, looked at the bear, and took off his backpack, setting it on the ground. "Sure, as long as he's sleeping," he said, waving his muscular arm in that direction. The bear was lying flat on the grasses and sedges, head resting on front paws, eyes shut. He was within striking distance of a college baseball player with a good, strong throw.

The creek was over a hundred feet wide, but I only needed to wade twenty or thirty more feet to be in the middle of dozens of live salmon. This stretch was a pool between two rapids. Small rocks and loose gravel covered the bottom, the perfect habitat for spawning sockeyes. Annually, millions of these fish migrate from the ocean to the rivers, creeks, and streams feeding Bristol Bay. This concentration represents the largest remaining sockeye run in the world and one of the most critical salmon fisheries on Earth.

Fish darted left and right as I crept farther out into the water. My eyes kept following one and then another as they dashed about. I often purchase sockeye to eat, and all of them probably hatched in the waters of the Bristol Bay drainage. I was having difficulty believing that I was here and that these fish, which had achieved an epic migration, were swimming around my legs.

Approximately ten thousand people live within the Bristol Bay watershed, an area larger than West Virginia. This part of Alaska includes twenty-five federally recognized Native American nations. Their livelihood is closely tied to the ecological health of this area, and subsistence salmon fishing provides more than half of their annual protein. They harvest salmon, cure it, and then eat it throughout the year. Glen's son

facing page |

Male sockeyes arrive first and defend good nesting sites. When females arrive, they pair and prepare to nest in the gravel.

told me that his family collected salmon every year, and he pointed to a small building on the grounds at Port Alsworth where drying racks cured the meat. State and federal regulations allow all Alaska residents to harvest salmon through subsistence permits.

A dorsal fin cut the water's surface just ten feet from me. One salmon closely followed another, probably a male courting a female that was being coy. This spot seemed like a perfect place to give photography a try. I fiddled with my phone, finding the camera app and video mode, and then dropped my hand into the cold water.

After a minute, I raised my phone to my chest, and someone from the shore yelled, "How's the water?"

A male follows a female sockeye as she prepares to build a redd for her eggs. The pair will release eggs and sperm simultaneously above the depression. The fertilized eggs settle into the gravel.

"Wonderfully wet!" I hollered. It wasn't as cold as I had expected. Snowbanks fed this creek but not glaciers. It thus wasn't hard to keep my hand in the water. Quickly, I played the clip. A male sockeye swam through the frame, its elongated jaw with a hook on the end (called a kype) showed prominently. The soft afternoon light made the sockeye's bright red skin gleam.

I didn't notice whether he had grown teeth. Sockeyes' jaws become elongated just before breeding, and the fish develop long, sharp teeth. This sockeye was big, more than two feet long, and looked incredibly lively, flicking his caudal fin slightly to zip out of my frame. In response to a yell from the shore, I waved my phone to indicate success and then dipped it in again.

A male sockeye swims near a female. Males develop a hooked beak and teeth as they approach breeding conditions.

Three sockeyes lurked in front of my submerged phone, while two others moved behind me. Their skin glistened and made me want to snorkel with them. That would've meant more equipment to carry, though. I thought about how my body had changed as I aged. Amazingly, these fish had undergone a remarkable transformation since they left the saltwater of Bristol Bay just one month ago. In the ocean, the salt in the surrounding water causes their bodies to dehydrate, but the opposite happens once they enter the fresh water to migrate upstream. Their bodies absorb water through their gills. In the marine world, they drink copious amounts of water and have a highly developed salt gland that helps them regulate their electrolytes. In freshwater, they stop drinking and instead continuously pump out urine. These changes are rapid and critical for their survival. My body's changes have been slow, with a gradual reduction in fitness and an increase in weight—neither of which are good for survival.

One sockeye, a male, drifted within a few feet of my hand, and I thought about lunging for him, just like a bear, but my fingernails were trimmed short. Incredibly, these fish stop feeding when they leave the ocean, fueling their migration with fat reserves. Subconsciously, my other hand poked my belly. Even through my waders, I could feel my substantial fat reserves. My problem is that cooking, eating, and entertaining are fun, so I do too much of them. Remarkably, the digestive systems of salmon regress, making room for more eggs or sperm. Their flesh becomes pale in color and mushy in texture and doesn't have a good flavor, at least not to humans. The pink of their flesh comes from the carotenoids in their marine food. They migrate to the fish's skin, changing it from the silvery color of the ocean-going sockeye to bright red.

I scraped my feet back and forth in the gravel, studying the pebble size and water flow. Salmon use Earth's magnetism as an internal GPS unit and their sense of smell to guide them to their natal stream bed, where they will spawn. Some of these fish seemed to have set up territories. Proper gravel size and streamflow for keeping the eggs oxygenated are critical. Males arrive first. The strongest ones defend the prime sites. Too much flow might wash the eggs downstream, and too little might cause them to suffocate before hatching. These pebbles seemed perfect, providing crannies into which the eggs could settle.

My fingers started getting cold, so I stood to look around, switching hands for the phone and sticking the cold one in my vest for a few seconds. Some of the red blobs seemed paired up. The female picks a place to lay her eggs and excavates a depression in the gravel by turning on her side and fanning her tail.

That would be fun to watch, and again, I wished I had a snorkel. The depression—the nest—is known as a redd. A dominant male then shadows her, which was what I was seeing around me. She's ready to spawn when she touches her anal fin to the gravel. The two come side by side and simultaneously release the eggs and sperm above the redd. Anywhere from a few thousand to ten thousand eggs could be deposited in a single nest. The fertilized eggs settle into the gravel. The pair may move upstream and repeat the process. The parents die, and a new generation hatches in a few months.

The pair swam in a circle, not twenty feet away. They will die soon after their eggs are fertilized and before the young even develop. These parents will never see their offspring, the next generation. This made me think of Ann. She had wanted to see our daughter graduate from college, marry, and become independent—well, maybe not the independent part. But she was diagnosed with ovarian cancer when Kelsie was just nineteen. It was a non-tumor-forming cancer impossible to detect until it had spread throughout her body. The prognosis was never good, but she desperately wanted to be around to see a grandchild. Over the next thirty months, especially when things weren't going well, she would occasionally talk about wanting to hold that grandchild or see Kelsie graduate. Even when I took Ann to the hospital for the last time, she was still fighting. Midway through Kelsie's senior year in college, Ann died. She would have been proud of our daughter, now married and living in Australia. Perhaps I could have, should have done more.

A splash startled me as a pair of sockeyes swam off. Wondering if I could find a place where a pair of sockeyes was about to spawn, I shuffled to another spot. Being in knee-deep water with dry feet and legs was a strange sensation. I hadn't worn waders since graduate school, when I used them to study nesting colonies of boat-tailed grackles. The grackles nested in cattail marshes, and I waded through the cattails, recording information on their breeding biology, always on the lookout for alligators, which frequented those Florida ponds. The bear was still sacked out; it hadn't moved.

That morning, we had hiked about a mile farther down Funnel Creek to spend time by a five-foot waterfall. Thirty or more sockeyes lingered in a deep pool just below the falls, waiting for the right moment to jump the cascade. Perhaps they were resting, building up energy for the leap. The drive to migrate seems unbelievable. Yes, it's all about reproduction, but the physical challenge of running up rivers is still monumental.

The sockeyes around me had likely hatched here a half decade ago. The fry had perhaps spent a year or so in freshwater before leaving for saltwater as small smolts, weighing only a few ounces. For several more years, they must have fed, swimming over a vast area of the North Pacific, from the Gulf of Alaska through the Aleutian Islands and across the Bering Sea, before starting the arduous migration back to this spot. They must have grown on all those marine nutrients, gaining weight until they weighed ten pounds—maybe fifteen.

Sockeyes congregate at the base of a small waterfall. Here, they rest before attempting to climb the cascade.

These fish make a perfect meal for bears that need to build up fat. Bears have a drive to fish even if they aren't hungry. Earlier, back at the falls, we had watched one catch a salmon after a long chase, but he didn't start eating it immediately. Instead, he played with it. The bear had the salmon's tail in its mouth and began to whip it around like a ball at the end of a string. Someone joked that it must have been mad about having caught a male salmon instead of a female full of roe. Bears want as many nutrients as possible, and they prize roe and skin fat.

The brown bear whips its catch back and forth, playing with it like a ball on a string.

Ensuring that enough salmon migrate up these rivers to spawn and feed the bears is critical to this ecosystem. Humans have developed incredibly effective techniques for capturing fish, especially those that funnel out of saltwater and up rivers. Nets, traps, and seines are efficient in that they allow people to take every single salmon before any can reach freshwater. In Washington, this was a significant problem in the nineteenth and twentieth centuries, and the unregulated commercial fleet almost wiped out many salmon runs. Fortunately, the Bristol Bay fisheries are highly regulated, and the Alaska Department of Fish and Game is charged with ensuring that harvests are sustainable. In 2018, fishermen caught 219 million pounds in Bristol Bay, 57 percent of the world's catch of sockeye salmon. The Alaska Department estimated that forty million sockeyes might attempt the run in 2019. Therefore, they would permit a commercial harvest of twenty-seven million fish, allowing about twelve million—some of these right here—to migrate up the rivers to spawn.

Twelve million salmon seems like a lot spread through the nine rivers that drain into Bristol Bay, but that's only a third of what might swim into freshwater if humans didn't harvest them. I scanned the surface around me and counted three or maybe four dozen fish within a pebble toss. If there were no human catch, might there have been more than a hundred here? Salmon gain much of their weight in the marine environment, bringing ocean nutrients up rivers. Bears depend on those nutrients for annual weight gain; many other organisms need them to survive and prosper. In Alaska, glaucous-winged gulls follow the salmon up the rivers. Each time a bear catches a fish, the gulls swarm around it, waiting for scraps. Once the bear leaves the carcass, they move in like a horde of elementary school children after free candy. Bald eagles, common ravens, and American crows also pick over scraps from bears, as do several other mammals.

facing page |

Glaucous-winged gulls lurk near a brown bear, waiting for salmon scraps.

Three harlequin ducks rest along Funnel Creek. These ducks feed on aquatic insects whose abundance is enhanced by the nutrients from salmon carcasses.

The nutrients, however, feed the whole food web, boosting its productivity. When there was a lull in bear activity near the falls, I watched three harlequin ducks make a looping circuit along a quarter-mile stretch of the creek. These birds feed on aquatic insects and actively forage underwater, often in swift-moving flows. They repeatedly dove into the pool just below the falls, and I wondered what midges or fly larvae they might find. The trout here also benefit from the increased production of algae, zooplankton, and invertebrates that salmon carcasses bring. Salmon fry feed on aquatic insects that are probably more abundant in this creek and more nutritious because of the marine nutrients.

A partially eaten sockeye lays in the shallows of Funnel Creek. Sometimes, bears only eat the best parts and leave the rest. Nutrients from decaying fish fertilize the ecosystem. A few salmon eggs nestle in the gravel behind the fish.

Ecologists have shown that salmon nutrients fertilize the terrestrial systems near streams, particularly the riparian habitat. Most of the bears along Funnel and Moraine Creeks carry their catch onto the tundra and pick it apart there. They roam the hills between their fishing episodes and deposit their waste daily. We stepped over numerous scat piles on our hikes back and forth. Research in the Pacific Northwest has shown that salmon nutrients increase the growth rates of trees, bushes, and other plants along streams. The sedges, grasses, and blueberries we watched bears eat here were probably more abundant and more nutritious because of the salmon carcasses.

One salmon cruised right toward my leg and darted away with a snap of its tail. Watching the salmon zip by made me think of the proposed Pebble Mine. For much of the last twenty years, Native Americans, commercial fisheries, environmental groups, and many Alaskans have challenged this proposal because it threatens the continued viability of these sockeye runs. A foreign company wants to make an open-pit mine north of Iliamna Lake in the Kvichak and Nushagak River systems. The Environmental Protection Agency (EPA) ruled against the company in 2014 because of the mine's ecological dangers. In the gravelly lands of this part of Alaska, surface and groundwater contamination would be a certainty.

Furthermore, if the mine were to be built, someone would need to manage the tailings, wastewater, and toxins from the operation forever. The likelihood of a containment failure at some point, releasing millions of tons of toxins into the environment, is almost guaranteed. The *Washington Post* summarized the EPA's findings as follows: "A large-scale mining operation in Alaska's Bristol Bay would destroy a significant portion of the watershed, a pristine fishery that supports nearly half the world's sockeye salmon and dozens of Native villages that have relied on fishing for thousands of years." Yet, the Trump administration revoked the EPA's determination, removing its jurisdiction and turning the project's approval over to the Army Corps of Engineers.

Over 80 percent of the residents in the Bristol Bay region oppose the mine, and over 85 percent of the bay's commercial fishing industry also rejects it, as does the vast network of chefs who depend on this area for their salmon. The EPA made its determination based on an extensive scientific analysis of the environmental threats and had its assessment thoroughly peer-reviewed, twice. Yet, the Trump administration abandoned the EPA's restrictions and implemented a fast-tracked process designed to approve the mine before the end of Trump's first term as president. The problems this mine would pose for salmon and Southwest Alaska are extensive.

The brown bear grabs a mouthful of blueberry branches and then pulls up, stripping the berries from the twigs.

The Trump administration ignored science because its values lay elsewhere. I was terribly naïve when I started my career. I thought that if I did good, defensible science, it would influence policy, helping to protect the environment and restore degraded ecosystems. I thought that I needn't worry about the policy because science would drive it. However, after spending a decade researching South Florida's ecosystems, I discovered that it was essential for scientists to enter the fray of policy development. They needed to be vocal advocates of what their science meant and, therefore, what the policies should be. I then moved to Washington, DC, to work at the science–policy interface, first for The Wilderness Society and then for the National Audubon Society. Policies reflect our society's values, which depend on people caring. This now seems to be where my energies are focused. Maybe my career was the reverse of what it should have been.

The problem for sockeyes is that they are a long way from most people in the United States—out of sight and, therefore, out of mind. The Trump administration's values lay in making the most money possible for its friends. Apparently, the day after the owner of the Pebble Mine visited an official in Washington, DC, the federal government's goal became the approval of this mine—consequences be dammed.

facing page |

Along Funnel and Moraine Creeks, brown bears actively chase down sockeyes. They will pursue a fish for a dozen seconds or more, running through knee-deep water. High levels of heavy metals, such as copper, might affect the salmon's ability to escape bears.

Numerous salmon mingle in the shallows as they pair and find the right nesting spot. A brown bear walks through the swarm, paying no attention to them.

Two sockeyes swam right by my leg, as if I were simply a stump in the water. Perhaps I would have felt their tail flicks if I hadn't been wearing thick waders. They were oriented toward the task of reaching their spawning location. However, high concentrations of copper are known to disrupt salmon in various ways that might decrease their survival and navigation abilities or make them more susceptible to predation.

Copper is a tricky element. It naturally occurs in low concentrations and is a trace metal necessary for the growth and metabolism of all living organisms. In higher concentrations, though, it's deadly. At levels not much above the level needed for the growth and reproduction of freshwater fish, copper becomes toxic to them. High concentrations can reduce salmon's sense of smell and disrupt the functions of their lateral lines. The lateral line runs down a fish's side and helps it detect vibrations, water flow, and what's happening around it, playing a critical role in its orientation, schooling, and predation avoidance. Disruption of their lateral lines might decrease salmons' ability to avoid being caught by bears, and loss of smell might limit their ability to find their native spawning places. The mining process would release vast amounts of copper.

High copper levels are also toxic to unicell algae, the base of the salmonid food chain. With reduced algae production, there would be fewer zooplankton in the water. Juvenile sockeyes spend one to two years in freshwater, feeding primarily on zooplankton. These little organisms are also negatively affected by high levels of copper, which cause their populations to decrease. In addition, a slew of other heavy metals released by mining processes would increase the mortality of all these organisms.

One argument of the mine's proponents insisted that it would provide good-paying jobs for the locals. Based on Western economic measures, some would say that people here live in poverty. We asked Glen Jr. for his thoughts about the mine and the local population. His immediate concern was that the mining

Some sockeyes are paired and looking for nesting locations while others continue the journey to their natal areas, where they will spawn.

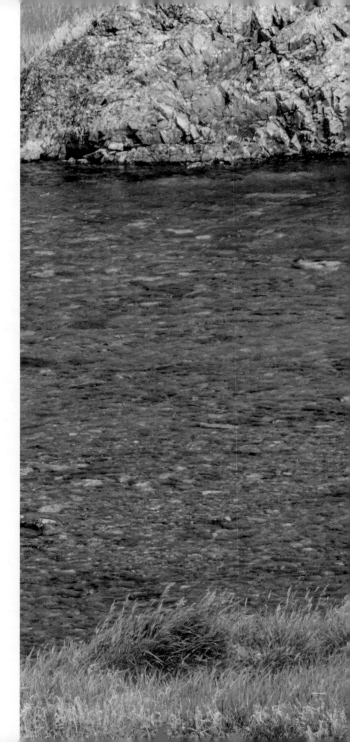

company would not finance or be able to clean up any pollution that might damage the ecosystem. His livelihood depends on a healthy ecosystem. His discussion of jobs was interesting. The mining company would likely expect workers to show up daily for an eight-to-five job and have zero tolerance for no-shows. However, the local population's culture is dependent on subsistence. Over thousands of years, people needed to respond to excellent opportunities to fish or hunt. This determined their survival. Glen said that most locals would lose their jobs relatively quickly, and outsiders would likely staff the fully developed mine.

Furthermore, the influx of outsiders would contribute to the destruction of the Native culture. When the mine closed, the outsiders would depart, leaving the locals with a devastated landscape, a destroyed culture, and unimaginably bad social conditions. Maybe the economists who focus on indices of happiness and social values have a point against those who focus only on indices centered on money.

The permit application said that the company would capture and treat the leachate, but the EPA estimated that 99 percent would need to be caught and processed to maintain the water quality. With the porous nature of the ground—high in gravel and sand—this seems unlikely. As these dams are projected to be up to 685 feet tall, the occurrence of a break or massive spill is not unimaginable.

Heavy rains or earthquakes would stress the structures and their capacities. The EPA analysis showed that substantial wastewater leakage or the accidental release of wastewater or tailing sludge would destroy many salmon areas far downstream and would affect the culture of Native Americans who depend on these salmon. The devastating effects could stretch through much of the Bristol Bay system. Although this place where I stood photographing salmon is outside the direct path of the proposed mine, fish returning here to Funnel Creek would have to swim through waters that could be influenced by mine runoff.

I looked across the landscape, thinking that if the mine were to be built, this area would still look pristine to the layman's eye, but the effects of heavy metals could easily influence life here. The salmon carcasses would carry those poisons. My thoughts flew to Ann. Nine months after she died of ovarian cancer, I was diagnosed with prostate cancer and had the tumor removed. When I asked the doctor why I developed cancer, he casually said, "You were probably exposed to some toxin or carcinogen along the way." Ann's doctors didn't think her cancer was a result of some exposure, but there's now a lot of discussion around the effects of talcum powder, which she used for a decade or more. The damage from the mine might be invisible to many who would visit this area. I looked at my hand down in the water and wondered how we get more people to think about those consequences and see beyond the surface.

For decades, our approach to toxins in this country has been that they couldn't be regulated unless someone proved they were harmful to people. That seems backward to me. The administration's policies have been to relax or even roll back environmental regulations, allowing companies to release more pollutants into the air and water. Scientific analysis has clearly shown that the Clean Air and Clean Water Acts have saved lives, freed many people from suffering, and saved millions of dollars in healthcare costs for the country. The administration claims that its policies are about jobs, but they're really about profits—not people, animals, or happiness.

The owners and shareholders of the proposed mine don't live here in Alaska, don't depend on this landscape for their existence, and probably don't even know of the beauty of this country or its wild inhabitants. They're blind to the consequences of their mining operation, thinking only about the money they could make from it. I tugged on the top of my waders, thinking how dry and warm my feet seemed. The waders had done their job even though I'd mostly forgotten about them. The opposite may be true, however, when it comes to protecting the richness that is the Alaska wilderness. Ignorance of what's at stake may be the most important thing to conquer so we can stop the carpetbaggers who don't care.

My hands had been in the water for several minutes, photographing salmon swimming back and forth. They were definitely cold now. The video looked good, although in the middle I was pointing the camera at the bottom. I started back toward the shore. As I approached the edge, Glen walked briskly down toward me. "You better come out of the water now!" he said, his hands waving at me with urgency, signaling me to hurry. The bear was sitting up, looking back and forth. I scrambled up the bank's side and moved into the middle of our group. Just then, the bear stood, stretched, and marched out into the creek, where he immediately began chasing fish. The Natives of British Columbia called these salmon *suk-kegh*—redfish. Our inadequate pronunciation came up with "sockeye." At least for now, Funnel Creek was this bear's restaurant.

CHAPTER 5 | Sculpting

Our pilot, Carlon Voran, eased up on the yoke of the Cessna, and we glided along at four thousand feet, just barely above the mountains right in front of the plane. His hands rested lightly on the yoke as if he was just coaching the plane along. His well-trimmed brown beard accented his young face. As we had loaded the plane that morning, his comments increased my excitement about our planned excursion—he spoke so fondly of the volcanos and glaciers we would see. I craned my neck to look out the windshield and then pressed my head against the right window to look straight down. Snow and ice covered these mountains in Lake Clark National Park.

Half an hour earlier, we had left Port Alsworth and flown over Kontrashibuna Lake and up its central valley into the Chigmit Mountains, climbing steeply, the plane's engine straining. Filled with glacial water, Kontrashibuna Lake was turquoise blue. Suddenly, I realized that the valley was the large U-shape typical of those carved by massive alpine glaciers during the Pleistocene. The cut of the ice chisel must have gone a thousand feet up its sides. We flew low over these mountains, which were still being built by the subduction of the Pacific tectonic plate. Below us was evidence of our planet's ongoing geologic transformation, which included glaciers, snowfields, rugged mountains, and volcanoes. This flight today would give us a chance to look at the processes that continue to mold our planet.

Carlon now had us heading toward our first close look at glaciers. These rivers of ice have played a significant role in sculpting the landscape of North America, and the continent-wide glacial swaths of the Pleistocene have influenced the evolution of organisms by separating ancestral populations. I remembered reading in graduate school about how those successive glaciers may have divided ancestral populations of black-throated green warblers, resulting in the evolution of the complex that includes them and Townsend's, hermit, and probably black-throated gray warblers.

I understood the basic principles of glacier formation: more snow falls than melts. It's all about temperature; a slight change determines whether glaciers will grow or recede. I'm most familiar with the glaciers at Mount Rainier in Washington. They come from the top or sides of the mountain and flow down. In other places, these ice rivers come out of massive snowfields, which is how they form in Antarctica and Greenland. This process must also have driven the development of the continental glaciers. The Alaskan mountains below extended over an area large enough for us to find giant snowfields.

facing page |

Ospoock Creek flows into Kontrashibuna Lake. The blue water shows that this is a glacier-fed creek. Fine glacial flour gives it that color. The ice grinds rocks into sediment finer than sand grains. This flour material is suspended in the water.

Several hanging glaciers filled the window on my side of the plane as we climbed the valley. They flowed out of cirques carved into the mountain walls, extending to the edges of cliffs and sometimes lapping some way down a steep section. I couldn't take my eyes off one; it looked almost a square mile in size. Carlon turned the plane slightly to the left and said, "Look that way," pointing his long arm straight over the dash.

There, snow and ice extended at least three miles into the distance and more than a mile from side to side between rocky peaks on the left and a substantial rise on the right. It turned out that a big snowfield also went up that rise. The top must have covered six square miles, all snow. I thought, "So this is what a snowfield looks like," thinking of my Pennsylvania boyhood, where we tobogganed down the big hill, an area of four or five acres. The plane weaved back and forth. My head was plastered against the window, and my views were incredible. Glaciers poured out through every little depression in all directions. Straight in front of us was what looked like a river of ice heading down the valley. Tipping his head in that direction, Carlon said, "That glacier feeds the Tuxedni River. It flows into Cook Inlet." We had crossed the divide between watersheds that flow east or west.

facing page |

Permanent snow fills depressions on the tops of these mountains. The snow will eventually turn to ice and begin to flow, making small glaciers. Two hanging glaciers (center) emerge from the top snowfield.

As a glacier curls around a corner, the ice is twisted, forming intricate designs.

Here, more snow falls than melts each year. New snow buries last year's snow, compacting it and squeezing the air from between the crystals. After two winters, the snow becomes what glaciologists call firn. Firn is an intermediate state between snow and ice. Over time, the firn recrystallizes into ice and grows denser for up to one hundred years. The weight of the ice on a slope causes it to slide slowly, forming a glacier.

The plane was only a hundred feet above the ground, and we could see every detail in the snow and cracked ice. Carlon's eyes were glued on what was ahead of us; his hands lightly gripped the yoke. We dove down between ridges. He was taking us right along the glacier itself. I wished I could see the views from both windows at the same time.

At the height of the Pleistocene, glaciers covered 33 percent of the land and 30 percent

The thin rock ridgeline is known as an arête. Glaciers on both sides carve the rocks into these ridges.

of the oceans. Now, they comprise about 10 percent of the land and very little of the oceans. The Pleistocene sea level was several hundred feet lower because of all the water tied up in the ice. Ice sheets extended through Canada and into the northern parts of the continental United States. One lobe flowed down through Seattle to just below Olympia, Washington. The location of my house in North Seattle probably had a thousand feet or more of ice covering it only fifteen or sixteen thousand years ago. I had seen moraines, glacial erratics, and deep grooves in bedrocks left by these ice sheets, but their magnitude and influence on Earth remained hard to comprehend. Just a slight lowering of the world's temperatures caused these massive ice sheets to grow.

The plane's left wing dipped and gave me an incredible view to the right. I suddenly realized I was looking at an arête, a term I had read about before the trip—a line of rocks projected above the ice that flowed on both sides. Glaciers had carved this thin ridge of jagged rocks—the arête. As the plane banked more to the left, I noticed dark lines running down the middle of the glacier. These lines form where two glaciers come together. Both ice sheets had dragged rocks along their sides, the rubble looking like a median between lanes in a road. Our pilot circled up into a side glacier with this rock rubble through the middle of it and then looped back to head farther down this glacier toward the Tuxedni River. At least six smaller glaciers had come together, and the valley walls squeezed them. I sucked in air at that point, causing the pilot to ask if I was okay. "I'm fine, sorry," I said. I was trying to grasp how much pressure that ice must apply to the valley's sides. Six glaciers compressed into a width that one could cover. It made me think of scrubbing pots and all the elbow grease that goes into getting the stick off.

We climbed the western ridge of the valley to head north. Mount Iliamna rose to the southeast. These mountains are part of the Ring of Fire, the twenty-five-thousand-mile horseshoe of volcanoes and earthquake faults bordering the Pacific. Here was evidence of plate tectonics, a geologic phenomenon that continues to shape the world yet is hard to comprehend. The time frames in which this arc has sculptured the land are in millions, if not tens of millions, of years. These mountains rose in only the last twenty-five million to forty million years. However, even in recent times, there has been activity of monumental proportions.

A hundred miles or so south of here, the most massive volcanic eruption in the twentieth century took place. In 1912, Novarupta exploded, sending an estimated fifteen cubic kilometers of magma and ash into the air. The explosion was thought to be greater than that of Krakatoa. A foot of ash fell on an area the size of Delaware and Rhode Island combined. The dust apparently depressed world temperatures. The Novarupta eruption created the Valley of Ten Thousand Smokes, a forty-square-mile area covered with fumaroles, showing that there was molten rock not far below the surface. Novarupta is now just a bump in the valley, with a lava dome rising about two hundred feet. Steam still climbs from it.

While we were circling above the turquoise waters of Crescent Lake, I spotted an enormous glacier coming north from Mount Iliamna. Though a long way off, it was clearly several miles wide and extended for a good twenty miles from the volcano's summit before petering out near the Tuxedni River. This glacier was the most massive one I had ever seen. It might have been like the ones coming off Mount Rainier during the Pleistocene. Many

facing page |

A large glacier flows down from Mount Iliamna. This volcano is unstable and has had several major landslides in recent years.

were dozens of miles long and a thousand feet thick. At Mount Rainier, I like to hike Sourdough Ridge and Burroughs Mountain. Lava created them when it spilled from the volcano between two Pleistocene glaciers.

All the ridges above Crescent Lake showed the scars of past glaciers. Some still had ice at the top of their cirques. Broken rocks filled some cirques. The snow and ice were disappearing, and these glaciers had shrunk. In my lifetime, average world temperatures have increased by more than 1.5 degrees Fahrenheit, and the rate is accelerating. Projections suggest that the average world temperature will increase four to seven degrees more in the twenty-first century.

Greenland's ice sheet is melting at four times the rate that it did just fifteen years ago. Studies in Washington have shown a general shrinking trend. University of Washington Assistant Professor David Shean, PhD, estimated that Mount Rainier's glaciers had lost nine hundred million cubic yards of ice in the last fifty years. These glaciers currently cover thirty-five square miles. Shean's work suggests that if the ice were removed evenly across all the glaciers, it would be like slicing twenty-five feet off their thickness. That is equivalent to a two-story building. The scrapes and rock debris below many of the cirque glaciers here in Alaska suggest that they too have receded in recent years.

facing page |

When Mount Redoubt erupted in 2009, a massive lahar ripped down this valley toward Cook Inlet.

The altimeter read ninety-five hundred feet; we had climbed and were flying right toward Mount Redoubt. Carlon's eyes were fixed forward; maybe we could look down into the crater. This volcano erupted in 2009, shooting an ash cloud into the stratosphere that later drifted east over Alaska and Canada. On the western side, the summit was a shallow U-shape. Steam rose from just beyond the rim, between the two ridges. As we came around the northwest side, clouds draped the slopes, but they were light and fluffy compared to the darker, denser steam.

A steaming lava dome rises in the middle of Mount Redoubt. This volcano erupted in 2009. In the distance is Mount Iliamna, another volcano in the Pacific's Ring of Fire.

"See that black mound? That's the lava dome," Carlon said, pointing to the black rock pile in the middle of the crater. It was steaming. I could see that the eruptions had blown out this side of the peak.

The lava dome was a few hundred feet high but still below the ridges circling the summit. To the south, Iliamna rose above the mountain chain; and to the north, Mount Spurr, another volcano, stuck out.

Carlon began a big circle to the left. Ash from Redoubt's last eruption had blanketed a glacier that ran down toward Cook Inlet. That eruption also released a massive lahar that ripped down the north slope, through the Drift River Valley, and toward Cook Inlet. Much like liquid cement, a slurry of ash, rocks, water, and ice—maybe one hundred feet thick—had rushed along at sixty miles per hour. Anything in the way—plant or animal—would have been killed.

A volcano rose from this mountain six hundred thousand to nine hundred thousand years ago. The volcano is now extinct, replaced by Mount Redoubt. The ice river is a branch of Double Glacier.

North of the Drift River, we started to fly over yet another vast snowfield. Small rock peaks stuck through the white all across it, but the snow extended for miles in several directions. Double Glacier, Carlon called it, named after the two massive branches of ice that flowed down toward the Drift River. The mountain was the remnant of an extinct volcano that had been active at the height of the Pleistocene, six hundred thousand to nine hundred thousand years ago. The size of the snowfield that fed those two glaciers impressed me; it was far bigger than anything I had ever seen, including earlier on that flight. The maps I later studied suggested that the snowfield might have extended over almost one hundred square miles,

larger than Seattle. I tried to conceive of an area from my house almost to Seattle's airport, covered in snow and ice hundreds of feet thick.

We think of stratovolcanoes as permanent, but they're relatively short-lived, geologically speaking. Volcanoes like Mount Rainier exist for about a million years. Mount Rainier is about five hundred thousand years old now. The lava and ash cones erode as they die, but a new volcano pushes up from the mantle if continental drift continues. I saw the young Mount Redoubt, which had succeeded the now-extinct volcano under Double Glacier here in Alaska. Perhaps the cone of Double Glacier once rose thousands of feet above these mountains. Might it have been much taller than Redoubt?

This undulating snowfield feeds the Shamrock Glacier. Here, more snow falls than melts, gradually becoming ice.

Our plane continued north, crossing the North Fork Big River, up over a ridge, and looping over a lake filled with icebergs. The Blockade Glacier flowed down from the northern mountains into this valley, where it fanned in both directions, creating a giant dam. Beyond the downstream end of the ice, the McArthur River flowed toward Cook Inlet, but on the upstream side, the ice blocked the water. It made me think of the Missoula floods that carved the Columbia Basin. A lobe of ice blocked the North Fork River in Idaho, creating Lake Missoula—more than two thousand feet deep—behind it. The ice dam formed and broke more than forty times over two thousand years or so, each time causing a cataclysmic flood across Central Washington. Here was that concept in miniature.

The previous spring, I had stood at the edge of a three-hundred-foot-high cliff in Washington's Columbia Basin. Frenchman Coulee stretched before me a mile or longer and a half mile wide. Those successive floods out of Lake Missoula carved it from the Miocene lava flows. Now, here in these Alaskan mountains, I was still trying to fathom the geologic time and the sculpting of our landscape. These mountains in Alaska have risen in the last twenty million years or so, and glaciation and erosion have sculpted them. The moving tectonic plates are still molding what's here, but at a speed we can't easily comprehend.

Seeing a glacier from a few dozen feet above is incredible. Our pilot flew the Cessna back and forth over this glacier to give us magnificent views of the ice, its patterns, and its textures.

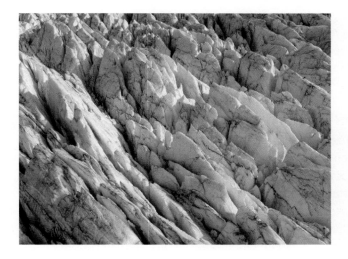

Glacial ice can be hundreds of years old. This ice, along the Shamrock Glacier, shows the cracking that comes with movement and the weathering caused by exposure.

A medial moraine shows where the two branches of the Shamrock Glacier come together.

Carlon interrupted my thoughts when he extended his arm in front of me and said, "Shamrock Glacier." We had passed over the next ridge and were approaching a massive glacier. It was at least a mile wide. The plane did a complete circle over the head of Shamrock, and then Carlon dropped it down so we were only thirty feet above the snow and ice. He started flying a lazy zigzag down the glacier, the way a skier might weave down a slope. I had terrific views up and down the ice. Massive crevasses zigzagged across the structure. From the backseat, Dan said, "If you fall in one of those, it's all over." As the ice shifts, crevasses open and close, crushing anything trapped there. Halfway down the mountain, the other branch of the Shamrock Glacier came in from the east, and the two compressed into a valley no broader than each had emerged from. Large lateral moraines, a hundred or more feet high, were pressed on both sides of the valley. Not long ago, this glacier had been much thicker.

The ice dissolved into a lake near the mouth, and rock piles littered the area. A several-hundred-foot-high terminal moraine formed a 270-degree loop from both sides of Shamrock's valley, creating a dam for the lake. An opening to the east allowed water to flow into Chakachamna Lake; upstream of the moraine was Kenibuna Lake.

I sat in awe; this was the evidence of the Little Ice Age I had hoped we might see. Between 1250 and 1850, Earth cooled, apparently because the sun was a little less active then. Glaciers expanded, becoming thicker and moving farther down their valleys. Here, the Shamrock Glacier had come out of the valley, spread laterally, covering maybe five square miles, pushing vast mounds of rock in front of it. Scientists have discovered that during the Little Ice Age, most glaciers in different parts of the world varied in how long they grew. The glaciers here might have been the longest in the 1800s or in the late 1700s. The temperature then was only slightly lower than what humans experienced in the early twentieth century, yet it created massive problems for human civilizations.

The Little Ice Age caused crop failures and famine in much of Europe. Philipp Blom, in his book *Nature's Mutiny,* describes how the Little Ice Age shaped our Western culture. With less production, landlords kicked peasants out of farms, which led to an influx of people into the cities and then increased the poverty and social problems there. Some of the pressures that caused people to leave Great Britain, Ireland, and Europe and emigrate to the United States originated in these famines and the unrest that followed them. Social systems were in a state of chaos: capitalism expanded, and societies changed, all due to a slight temperature change.

The Little Ice Age may have been a driver of my ancestors' move to the United States. My paternal side left England in the 1640s, and my maternal side left Germany in the 1870s. The immediate reasons for their emigration are lost to history, but I wonder if the economic and social changes brought on by the Little Ice Age played a significant role. How far had the Shamrock Glacier advanced into this valley when each family climbed onto a ship bound for America?

A loop up the Nagishlamina River highlighted the importance of the Pleistocene and the Little Ice Age. They both helped define the world as we now know it. The valley was over a mile wide, flat across the bottom, and lush green on my flight. A Pleistocene glacier had carved this valley, and that ice must have been over a thousand feet thick. It receded, disappearing sometime in the last ten thousand years or so. Then, in the previous millennium, the Harpoon Glacier expanded from its valley into the Nagishlamina River, creating the moraine we now looped around. What fascinated me was how the climates that drove these ice expansions and retreats had influenced human evolution and culture.

The climate that caused the Pleistocene glaciation was a primary driver of human evolution. It influenced the vegetation and food supplies on the plains of Africa. Anthropologists have postulated that our ancestral populations went through a

facing page |

The Shamrock Glacier formed this terminal moraine during the Little Ice Age. Glaciers expanded from about AD 1250 to the late 1800s, and the Shamrock came out of its valley, piling a mound of dirt before it.

severe reduction in size about seventy thousand years ago, when Earth had cooled. The warming that caused these vast glaciers to recede—such as the one that carved the Nagishlamina Valley—set the stage for human migration worldwide, including across the Bering Strait and into North America. It probably also contributed to our shift from hunter-gatherers to agriculturists.

Then, in the last millennium, the Little Ice Age brought havoc to European culture; crop failures and the resulting famines drove enormous social change. European society shifted from a focus on monarchy and religion to what became known as the Enlightenment. The middle class began to rise, and individual rights and freedoms began to grow—if you were in the right group. Our economics became focused on continual growth by exploiting Earth's resources. Huge emigrations to the Western Hemisphere took place, and Europe attempted to dominate and exploit Africa, Asia, Australia, and the Americas. The climate of the Little Ice Age probably affected people, their social systems, and cultures across the globe, not just in Europe. All this happened because of a slight decrease in temperature. In the twenty-first century, however, we see global temperature going in the opposite direction.

A Pleistocene glacier carved the Nagishlamina Valley. The flat bottom and steep, rounded sides are typical of valleys that have been sculpted by thick alpine glaciers.

Now, we have the scientific method, much data looking backward, and the ability to develop predictive models, but as a human race, we seem unable to make changes based on what science tells us. In the twenty-first century, the world is warming because we are burning fossil fuels, and these changes negatively affect our civilization. Yet, the entire United States society seems to be slinking backward, away from science, and more toward fear, isolation, and falsehoods. When the Little Ice Age began, famine, hardship, and suffering were thought to emanate from God's wrath at humans' wrongdoing—in other words, divine punishment. These same views are harbored by some sectors in the United States as we deal with severe weather events, droughts, wildfires, hurricanes, and, recently, a pandemic.

Although we like to think of the United States as the greatest nation on Earth, in the spring of 2020, we had the highest rates of infection and death from COVID-19 of any country in the world. Many think this is because our administration, many state leaders, and our Senate scorned science and focused instead on blustering about the virus's threat. They seem more interested in protecting the wealth of the few while letting the many suffer. We might still have time to reverse the effects of global warming. To accomplish this, we may have to shift our mindset away from exploitation and continuous economic growth.

These ruminations make me think of my daughter in Australia and the world she will inherit. They also make me think about time.

Isaac Newton was a remarkable individual. He thought of time as continuous and consistent in pace and direction. Modern physicists consider time part of a four-dimensional complex known as the time–space continuum. Time is often further depicted as relativistic. Albert Einstein proposed this concept. He thought that time was relative to gravitational pull—the stronger the pull, the slower time goes. He postulated that a person high above Earth would age faster than one on Earth because time went faster in the former. His theory of relativity states that time and space are not immutable and fixed as they appear, and that time doesn't flow; it just is.

The mountains in Alaska have risen over the last twenty-five million years. Pleistocene glaciers and the cold spell of the Little Ice Age have carved them. Even now, continental drift, volcanic activity, and abiotic forces continue to mold these lands. For the last ten to twenty millennia, humans have lived in Alaska, adapted to its changes, and coexisted with the ecosystem, being part of it. But now, those in charge seem more focused on exploitation, both here and elsewhere, and all for short-term profits.

In April 2020, a pandemic had gripped the world. COVID-19 changed everything, shutting down the vast bulk of activity for the first few months. I left my house only to replenish food stores or walk in my neighborhood. In April, at the height of the pandemic, I had to return a microphone to a friend who lived five miles away. As I drove through Seattle's deserted streets, I felt like a high school student in the corridor without a hall permit. Contact with friends, family, and others was either electronic or at distances exceeding the wingspan of an eagle. I was unable to hug or be hugged by anyone for six weeks. Yet, the birds that came to my feeder continued to behave as they had for years. The Bewick's wren came daily and scolded me if I sat on my patio. The juncos were paired up and probably had a nest in one of my bushes. I dreamed of day trips or longer, to look for birds and hike in the wild.

The ancient Greeks had two concepts for time: Chronos and Kairos. Chronos is measured time, the way we typically think—in years, centuries, and millennia. My Alaska trip might have told me that I should think more in terms of Kairos, which means the perfect moment, the opportune time, the fleeting instant, the one that comes and goes in the blink of an eye.

Back on that day in August 2019, our plane gained altitude until we were above the mountains and headed back toward Farm Lodge. The rugged landscape extended in all directions, and a geologic fault ran through the valley directly below us. The Katmai Peninsula functioned in Kairos time.

Snowfields feed glaciers, which then carve the landscape. With climate change, glaciers are shrinking, pulling back up valleys and slopes, disappearing. This global issue affects all of us.

CHAPTER 6 | Turquoise

Carlon eased up on the throttle, and the Cessna began a slow glide. "Where are we headed?" I was in the copilot seat, and Mark and Dan were in the back. We had left Port Alsworth on Lake Clark a half hour earlier and were headed north along the western side of the Alaska Range.

"Turquoise Lake," Carlon said. "We will pass over it before flying on to Twin Lakes." I knew that glacial melt filled this lake, and it was reputed to be extremely beautiful. As a matter of fact, I could see it in the distance as the plane dropped to about four hundred feet, but my attention shifted to the tundra below. Audubon Alaska has designated these rolling knolls as an Important Bird Area because of the concentrations of several shorebirds that nested here. Moraines formed by a glacier created an undulating landscape covered with dwarf shrubs, lichens, and herbs—a perfect habitat for nesting birds. Significant numbers of American golden-plovers, surfbirds, Baird's sandpipers, and wandering tattlers are thought to nest here, and then there are also gray-crowned rosy-finches and northern wheatears. Conservation of this area is essential for these species.

facing page |

A Pleistocene glacier carved Turquoise Lake valley. Glacial till below the lake creates an undulating landscape filled with pools, and this area is perfect for nesting shorebirds.

Rolling hills have been carved and molded by Pleistocene glaciers. These areas are prime nesting locations for tundra-dependent birds.

I glued my eyes to the tundra, trying to spot any of the tiny birds as we zipped along. An Important Bird Area designation highlights the critical value that a place has for birds, but it doesn't bring any added protections for them. BirdLife International developed this tool, and Audubon has applied it in the United States. Seeing wheatears in North America would be a first for me, so I looked for a flash of white that might be the tail of one as it dashed from a branch. However, the tundra sped by, making it unlikely that I would detect any bird smaller than a goose.

The wandering tattler catches a fly on a barnacle-covered rock in Gray's Harbor. Tattlers nest in Alaska, including Katmai and Lake Clark National Parks, then migrate south, wintering along the west coast of the Americas or on islands in the Pacific.

Because of birds, I left a great job at The Wilderness Society to return to the National Audubon Society. Although our work at The Wilderness Society involved protecting habitats and influencing policies that affect them, the chief scientist position at Audubon would allow me to work directly on bird conservation, thinking about their needs and actions that might protect them. Before that transition, I noticed that eastern meadowlarks had disappeared from the countryside around our family farm in Pennsylvania. As a teenager, I watched them sing in the spring, as the hay began to grow, and they were around all summer, with a few staying through the winter. Analyses by National Audubon and the US Geological Survey showed that many common birds, including meadowlarks, have decreased in number since the 1960s. The reasons for this are complex and vary from species to species.

The Audubon position was a great opportunity for me, but within a month of my transition, my doctor suspected that I had prostate cancer. My prostate-specific antigen (PSA) levels had shot up in the previous year. He began a series of tests, including taking a tissue sample, which confirmed his suspicions. Bone scans revealed several hotspots that could be cancer tumors or scars from old bruises. Two dark nodes in my lungs sent me to consult the pulmonary specialist Ann had seen throughout her cancer ordeal.

I was scheduled for prostate cancer surgery a month later, and the doctors established a multi-year monitoring program for the bone and lung spots.

When I returned to work after a month of recovery from the surgery, my first responsibility was staff layoffs rather than bird conservation policy. The financial crisis of 2008 was in full swing, and Audubon needed to make substantial cuts. The surgery proved successful, and the monitoring showed no changes in the problematic spots or nodes over the next three years, giving me a cancer-free bill of health. My body seemed to relax at that news. Apparently, I had been under constant tension while waiting out that timeline. We still monitor the PSA level each year.

The plane hit a few bumps in the air, and I had to look toward the horizon to settle my stomach. Flying, especially in small planes has always been challenging for me. The tundra was a rich mixture of greens, reds, and browns. The afternoon light gave everything a warm hue. I realized that the plane was too fast and too high for me to notice any bird species, so I pushed myself to think about something positive. Many conservation strategies have been successful in my lifetime. The Turquoise basin is protected from development because it is in Lake Clark National Park, and this section is also a designated wilderness. However, Audubon's nomination of this basin as an Important Bird Area pointed out that threats to it still exist. If

A small creek runs through the tundra near Turquoise Lake. Numerous species of shorebirds nest in this area each summer.

the Pebble Mine materializes near Newhalen, air pollution might affect this area, and the human traffic to and from the mine might increase the disturbance. This part of the park is also within a military training zone for combat aircraft.

Even though this location is protected and—if the Pebble Mine project pushes through—the mining company might minimize threats through careful management of the mine and transportation, there's no guarantee that populations of these species will be stable. All the species are migratory, and there could be threats in other places that might jeopardize their status. In winter, the wheatears head west to Siberia and the

Eastern Hemisphere. The rosy-finches probably stay in Alaska but become nomadic, looking for good feeding areas, and the shorebirds head south along the coasts of North and South America. These migrants skip along their migration routes between breeding and wintering areas, stopping to refuel along the way. For migrants, protecting breeding, wintering, and stopover sites is essential. Some shorebirds show a high degree of site tenacity.

That thought reminded me of the great knots I had seen in Cairns, Australia. A study of this species highlights the importance of stopover places for migrants. My daughter and her husband live in Sydney, and I try to see birds on my visits. In 2015, I was walking along the esplanade in Cairns when twenty chunky, medium-sized shorebirds landed on a small sandbar just offshore. Grayish brown on their backs, whitish with speckling on their chests, and with medium-length bills, they looked a lot like the red knots of North America.

A study of this species showed what can happen if stopover places are lost. Numerous great knots winter in Australia and then fly north to their Arctic breeding grounds. They stop for a month or more to put on fat in the wetlands along the Yellow Sea, a body of water between the Korean Peninsula and China.

The extensive tidal flats bordering the Yellow Sea are rich in invertebrates. After flying several thousand miles nonstop, these knots must refuel, gaining weight to power their next leg north, toward the Arctic tundra. They nearly double their weight during a month of feeding in these mud-flats. Over the last several decades, the Chinese and Koreans have posed a survival challenge for shorebirds by implementing numerous "reclamation" projects involving draining tidal flats and converting them into dry lands for agriculture and development.

Over 30 percent of the world's great knot population historically staged in the Saemangeum on the east coast of South Korea. In 2006, Koreans completed a thirty-three-kilometer seawall in the Saemangeum that converted four hundred square kilometers of tidal flats—twice the size of Seattle—into dry lands and freshwater lakes. Before and after the closure, ornithologists coordinated extensive surveys throughout the Yellow Sea to determine whether the shorebirds that had foraged in the Saemangeum had gone elsewhere. They found no concurrent increase in great knot numbers in other foraging locations, suggesting that the individuals who historically fed in the Saemangeum had disappeared and probably perished.

Work in North West Australia confirmed this frightening discovery. Ornithologists in Australia predicted that, if great knots were faithful to their feeding areas in the Saemangeum, their studies should detect declines in North West Australia. By studying uniquely marked knots, ornithologists knew that individual birds were faithful to wintering sites, returning to the same place each winter, like a person who vacationed on the same beach yearly. Their surveys suggested that at least 80 percent of the ninety thousand birds missing from Korea had died. The scientists concluded, "This single reclamation project might have killed 20 percent of the world's population of great knots." Fortunately, South Korea has stopped all its reclamation projects along the coast and has focused on protecting the remaining feeding areas for shorebirds.

As I watched the great knots along the Cairns esplanade, the flock increased to more than fifty birds. Twos, threes, and fives would land and jostle for a position among the group. Some went to preening feathers, but most tucked their bills under their back feathers and closed their eyes.

They seemed content, probably because their stomachs were full and they were ready to rest.

I don't know of a similar study in the Western Hemisphere that shows what happens when stopover areas are lost. The tundra in Katmai may be protected from development and provide good breeding sites for the shorebird species that nest in Alaska, but these birds will also need good and safe feeding areas during their migrations and wherever they spend winter. Thus, vigilance beyond these protected areas is critical.

The Western Hemisphere Shorebird Reserve Network was established to highlight the importance of stopover areas. Gray's Harbor and Willapa Bay are part of this network in my home state. Protecting these areas will need constant attention as pressure mounts to expand shipping facilities and development along the shorelines. Sea-level rise and climate change continue to threaten this area.

Our plane glided along the valley, and thoughts of climate change made me stare down at this glacier-molded landscape. I had helped The Wilderness Society develop a multidimensional climate program, and I'd hoped to do something similar for Audubon. Instead, I fell into a state of despair and focused my attention on raising money for the staff in my department. In hindsight, that was a mistake; I should have concentrated more on building programs that could be integrated across the organization and with our international partners. My therapist thought that my depression was less about my job and more about my inability thus far to grieve Ann's death. She thought my move to Audubon was about postponing the realization that my wife would not return.

A pair of trumpeter swans caught my attention as the plane cruised over a small pond, and I smiled, thinking that conservation works. Remove the threat and birds will be resilient. In high school, I went with my sister Kitty to Yellowstone National Park; one of the species I wanted to find was this swan. In 1968, Yellowstone was one of only a few places in the lower forty-eight states where trumpeter swans lived, and we spent three days searching for them. Finally, I saw two floating in the water at a distance and through a thicket of small trees.

Because of market hunting, the known population of trumpeter swans dropped to less than seventy birds in 1939. These large birds were extensively hunted for meat and feathers in the late 1800s and early 1900s, decimating the wild population and reducing breeding to just a few places in the West. They are no longer hunted, and the species has recovered dramatically since that nadir. In 2015, ornithologists estimated that there were more than sixty thousand trumpeter swans in North America.

A pair of trumpeter swans glides low over my head and lands with a flock resting on Fir Island in Washington.

Looking back over my shoulder at two giant birds as the plane rushed on reminded me of a sighting in Washington last winter. The low-pitched trumpet came from behind where I stood on a dike in Skagit County. Turning, I spotted two large white birds that flew right overhead. Their translucent flight feathers glowed in the early morning sun. Their wingspan, more than six feet, created a moving shadow across Fir Island. Long white necks extended in front of solid bodies, and elephantine black legs and feet were tucked tight against their undersides. Over twenty-five pounds each, these trumpeter swans flew with grace, style, and dignity.

The pair circled the field a quarter mile east of my location, then set their wings, dropped their black feet, and landed without a stumble among several hundred swans. A few trumpets and calls drifted toward me from the crowd. Most, though, seemed to be resting on the green grass.

Now, many thousands spend the winter in western Washington and breed across the wilds of Alaska and Canada. Their recovery was hastened by their ability to adapt to new food sources. In winter, they graze heavily on grain fields and dig for spilled potatoes. The recovery of this species has always inspired me to keep working. Maybe some of these individuals that breed in the Katmai will come to winter in western Washington. I make an annual trek to the Skagit to watch these

magnificent birds and feel a sense of awe for them and their conservation.

As the swans disappeared from my small airplane window, my thoughts moved on to bald eagles. I had seen a few at Brooks Falls, but I thought we might have seen more along Funnel and Moraine Creeks. Maybe because there are no trees along those creeks, they don't go there to feed on salmon. This species is another success story for conservation and the Endangered Species Act. In high school, back in the late 1960s, several buddies and I would make an annual trek from our homes near Pittsburgh to Pymatuning Lake to look for a bald eagle. Only three pairs remained in western Pennsylvania, Ohio, western New York, and West Virginia, and only one of these pairs even attempted to breed. The culprit was the pesticide DDT and its derivatives. The pesticide builds up in the fatty tissue of animals and bioaccumulates as it moves up the food chain. Adult bald eagles had accumulated enough of this toxin that their eggshells were thinning, and when they tried to incubate their eggs, they cracked or crushed them. DDT was banned in the 1970s, and eagle populations have since slowly recovered.

On one of those Pennsylvania trips, we camped at the base of a peninsula that stuck out into Pymatuning Lake. The following day, we walked back through the woods toward the tip,

looking for an eagle. We didn't see one, but we did find a pair's nest. They continued maintaining the nest, adding new sticks each year, but apparently they hadn't laid any eggs in several years. I remembered looking up into the giant red oak at this massive bundle of interwoven branches. The structure was at least a human height thick and probably stretched an equal distance across. It reminded me of the tree houses in the movie *Swiss Family Robinson*, and I wondered what the view was like from up there.

Now, more than three hundred pairs nest in Pennsylvania alone, and a pair lives on the Allegheny River near my childhood farm. The number of breeding pairs in Washington has also steadily increased since 1970. Just before this trip, I watched several at Seattle's Union Bay, which is part of Lake Washington. Two adults were soaring overhead. Their long, rounded wings were flat, like a door, and the birds seemed to float effortlessly on them. The tips of their primaries were spread and turned slightly up, giving them added lift and superb control.

An adult bald eagle soars on long, rounded wings.

The banning of DDT allowed eagles to recover, and ending market hunting helped swans, but for many species, like eastern meadowlarks, no single thing seemed to have caused their decline. The National Audubon Society was part of a coalition of nonprofits, state and federal agencies, and local governments working to protect habitats and alleviate threats. As I emerged from despair, the Secretary of the Interior appointed me to a committee advising the Fish and Wildlife Service on regulations for siting wind farms. Wind energy production is critical to lessening our climate footprints. The turbines need to be sited where they might minimize bird and bat mortality. Audubon also worked on various policy issues, from agriculture to windows, urban sprawl, and climate change. In addition, I worked on integrating with BirdLife International's partners across the Western Hemisphere.

The work was exciting, and the coalition in the United States has now expanded its focus—under the mantra of "Bring Birds Back"—to include many actions that individual people can take to help recover bird populations. These involve planting native vegetation, reducing the use of plastics and pesticides, minimizing the danger posed by windows, and keeping domestic cats indoors. Conservation is making progress, and I have great hope for the future. Identifying the threats—like identifying my cancer—and then addressing them can work. Some things—like those spots on my lungs—aren't as scary as one might think but still require attention. A week before my Alaska trip, no PSA levels were detected in my blood eleven years after surgery. We can do this.

The plane slid out over the lake. The water—an intense mixture of blue and green—exuded calmness. Some say that turquoise symbolizes wisdom and creativity. As we recognize that no single conservation tool will save this planet's biodiversity, maybe humanity will become humble enough to give nature space to live.

facing page |

Small side streams flow into Turquoise Lake; the color of the silt in the streams contrasts with the bluish green waters of the lake.

CHAPTER 7 | Turning Points

It felt like coming home, although I had never been there. Even a year after that flight, I recall the whine of the engine as the Cessna banked at the east end of Upper Twin Lake. A tiny log cabin sat a short way back from the southern shore. The plane dropped to a few feet above the water and then set down gently, taxiing toward the beach. A thick boreal forest grew across the valley, and tundra ran up the steep slopes toward the mountain ridges. Several years ago, I read *One Man's Wilderness: An Alaskan Odyssey* by Sam Keith. The author used Dick Proenneke's journals to capture his story. At fifty-one, Dick had built this cabin, and he lived in it for nearly thirty years. He had chucked his busy work life to come to the wilds, not to conquer nature, but to be a part of it. Remarkably, Dick had used hand tools to build every piece of his cabin. He had captured the building process and his life in the wild with 8mm and 16mm movie cameras. When *Alone in the Wilderness*, the documentary incorporating those films, aired on the Public Broadcasting Service (PBS), I found it mesmerizing and bought a DVD copy of it.

Before alighting on Upper Twin Lake, Carlon had flown us up the Chilikadrona River toward Lower Twin Lake. Lake Clark National Park covers all these mountains and valleys. As the plane cruised at several hundred feet above the ground, my eyes watched the river; it was free-flowing and wild as it twisted back and forth across the broad valley bottom. I imagined Dick Proenneke hiking along its shore, a fishing rod over his shoulder, without a care in the world. Carlon tapped my shoulder and pointed over the dash. I stretched up high to look ahead. The valley was more than a mile wide, with U-shaped sides. A Pleistocene glacier had carved it. There, just ahead, was the lower lake and the outflow into the river. The summer that Dick built his cabin, Babe Alsworth flew him to Twin Lakes. They had to land on this one because ice still covered the upper lake.

facing page |

Dick Proenneke built this cabin with hand tools and lived in the wilderness along Upper Twin Lake for several decades.

Lower and Upper Twin Lakes extend most of the way across the U-shaped valley. Its contour indicates that a Pleistocene glacier carved it.

Consequently, Dick had to carry his gear 3.5 miles along the shore to his prospective homesite on Upper Twin Lake. It was May 23, 1968, a turning point in his life. He had mulled over whether he could do it—live there by himself and build a cabin. Apparently, he had been considering this change for some time.

As the lake became larger in front of us, I wondered about my fascination with Dick. Some of it probably relates to my being enthralled by wild countries and such. Dick had that same interest and went to live with it. I had always thought that when my career ended, I would buy a farm far from city life. But not long ago, I bought a house in Seattle, and it's likely to be where I'll live until I can no longer care for myself. Dick decided to upend his life, go in a new direction, and leave behind what he knew, and he did it consciously. My life ten years ago came to mind. It was difficult, and I was in a constant state of depression. Wild country played a central role in my recovery. But Dick was not depressed; he sought the wild on positive terms.

Carlon taxied up to the beach and jumped out, telling us to wait. He dragged the plane, pulling the tail up to the shore, and then returned for Mark, Dan, and me. My feet slid one way and then another in the one-inch-diameter rocks along the beach. These pebbles were like gigantic grains of sand. Dick carried buckets and buckets of them to make trails, the floor of his cabin, and a patio in front of it.

"Go on up the trail! I will tie up the plane!" Carlon called as he dragged a rope to a spruce tree. A ranger stood just outside the cabin, looking down the seventy-five-foot path at us. Ranger Kristin Dillon was young, maybe thirty, wearing the green uniform of the Park Service, with a broadbrim hat and a giant smile. She waved at us, signaling to us to come along.

The logs forming the walls of Dick's cabin were carefully hewn so that each was custom fitted to the one below.

The French door of Dick's cabin stood open invitingly. We formed a semicircle around Kristin, awaiting her instructions, but my eyes ran up and down the cabin. I had read about how Dick had custom-fitted each carefully hewn log end by tracing out a U on the upper log that matched the shape of the one below. He then removed the U with a saw, an axe, and a chisel. Each log was custom fitted to the next, so it was snug. The junctions looked solid, as if he had finished only yesterday, even though they had withstood this wilderness for nearly fifty years.

"Are you familiar with Dick Proenneke?" she asked. When we said we had seen the PBS special or read the book, she smiled and said, "Good." The cabin is a single room, eleven by fourteen feet, with a picture window looking onto Upper Twin Lake and a door pointing northeast. Thick moss grew on top of the roof. The ranger said that the Park Service had put a layer of new material under the moss to give the cabin better protection. Otherwise, everything remained precisely the way Proenneke had built it.

Evidently, two rangers shared the responsibility of guiding people through this landmark. Kristin was there for the summer, flying to the lake in late May and leaving in September, just before snowfall. On her days off, she canoed or hiked. She and her coworker lived in Spike Carrithers's cabin, five hundred yards up the lake. Spike introduced Dick to Upper Twin Lake by bringing him there one summer and offering him his cabin while he picked a spot and built his own. The setting spurred my dream of finding a remote site in the mountains where I could spend an extended period embedded in the wilds.

I don't think I'm drawn to the wilds for the same reason as Dick. According to Sam Keith, Dick wanted to test himself, wanted to see if he could handle the physical challenges of building a cabin and hiking in the wild by himself and the mental challenge of living alone for a year. Babe Alsworth would fly in with supplies every few weeks, so it was about something other than living off the land. According to Sam Keith, Dick contracted a severe case of rheumatic fever during World War II when he was in the navy, and this prevented him from being deployed to the South Pacific. He apparently considered this a failure of his body and wanted to prove that he had recovered.

I wasn't attracted to nature to prove something. It was the wild animals that drew me. At the age of five, I joined my sister Barbie, then eight, in catching minnows, crayfish, and salamanders in the hollow on our farm. We had a snake in a cage and a pet flying squirrel for a while too. By junior high, identifying birds and learning about their habits became my passion. I then studied birds in college and graduate school, moving first into scientific research and then into conservation. Wild places still draw me, inspiring in me a desire to identify still more kinds of organisms and see firsthand what I spent a career trying to protect. Last year, I even took a course about mosses and lichens. I think that naming organisms helps connect people to them, somehow making them more tangible and real. I want to take that concept further by believing that assigning a name to something helps people know it, recognize it, look for it, and care about it. Naming a thing allows us to see it more clearly and become more observant. A name acknowledges that an organism exists and engenders respect for it.

Helping others name species and recognize aspects of their lives has become central to my life. Maybe Mark's comments on the gulls helped me realize the importance of naming things; and now, at Dick's place, identifying things is again helping me think about my current life. In addition to naming birds, I tell stories about them, and people like that. Probably, it makes the species more real. The individuals we see take on new meanings, much like our friends. Friends are generally people we know a great deal about and whose lives we have learned to care about.

Moss grew thick on the roof of Dick's house. He carried giant sheets of it to cover the top of his house, as nature's insulation, and made a flat basket from sticks to haul them. He put tarpaper across the roof poles and then a polyethylene sheet to ensure that the water would run off. Snow would build on it, and the air trapped inside would keep the cold

winter out. The ranger saw the direction of my stare and said, "We have to water it to keep it lush and growing—one of our tasks." From the documentary, I remembered when Dick commented one winter's day that his home was toasty at forty-five degrees compared to the well-below-freezing temperature outside.

I looked closely at the doorframe just before ducking into the cabin. Enormous claw marks ran across the wood, and I recalled Dick's story of being stalked by a large grizzly. It had been lurking around his place, and he was becoming concerned about it. Finally, it chased him back into his cabin, where he shut and locked the door. He tried yelling, but the bear kept working on the cabin walls. He worried that if the bear climbed on the roof, it could easily tear through and get to him. So, Dick grabbed his rifle from over the fireplace and shot a few times out the big window, hoping to scare the beast away. It worked, but he wrote in his journals that he remained cautious after that.

Seeing those claw marks reminded me of a run-in I had with a bear. At sixty-one, I embarked on my first solo backpack hike, heading into Goat Rocks Wilderness in Washington's South Cascades. I left on a Tuesday, hoping that few people would be around for the next three days. No other vehicles were at the trailhead, which turned out to be at the end of an extremely bumpy nine-mile dirt road. I could occasionally hear truck traffic on US 12, but

A brown bear tried to claw its way into the cabin while Dick was inside.

the trip gave me the solitude I sought. About a mile along the trail, fresh elk footprints made me stop. Pressed onto a muddy spot, they were as big as my hand. This reminded me not to pitch my tent on a game trail. I found a lake and camped in the V of two large down logs several dozen yards up from the water. The evening was fantastic. Song sparrows, Swainson's thrushes, other thrushes, and Wilson's and Townsend's warblers sang all around me. Frogs began to call just as the sun set, and I went to sleep enjoying the anuran chorus.

I woke up screaming in the middle of the night. A black bear had both my ankles in its mouth. I was kicking as hard as I could, but I couldn't get my feet to separate. My knees were pulled up, and with each kick, my legs went only an inch or two down. The bear was gripping tightly. My arms were inside my sleeping bag, and I thrashed back and forth, trying to get them out, all the while hollering at the top of my lungs. Finally, I woke up, kicked a few more times, and then stopped while still gasping. Fortunately, it was only a dream, but it still scared me.

The forest was dead quiet, not a sound of any kind. My sleeping bag was wrapped around my legs, strapping my ankles tightly together, and I had slid partway down the tent, so my legs had to be bent halfway to my chest. I don't know why all that thrashing didn't break the end of my tent. I wiggled and peeled my way out of my sleeping bag, grabbed my headlamp, and peeked out the tent door. The forest was as I had left it the night before.

I staggered out in my stocking feet and stood beside my tent, shining my light in all directions. The lake was glass calm, and there was no movement in any trees or bushes. The air was fresh and clean, and everything was quiet. The frogs tuned back up a minute later and entered their full chorus. My dream had also scared them.

I ran my fingers across the claw marks on Dick's cabin door while thinking of those poor frogs in Washington. Inside Dick's place, the walls looked solid and strong, but that brown bear would have also scared the daylights out of me. Dick was alone and had to solve problems by himself, with no one to bounce ideas off or help him chase a bear away. Yet, that solitude still seemed enticing to me. I looked across his writing desk and out the large window onto Upper Twin Lake. Once, he had looked up from his desk and watched a moose and its calf walk by. Perhaps that's what solitude does for me—allows me to blend into nature, letting the wild surround me and function as if I didn't exist.

Sigurd Olson tells a story in *Reflections from the North Country* about a friend who took a weeklong canoe trip by himself although he usually went into the wilds with companions. The canoeist said it allowed him to spend as much time as he wished watching a family of otters, climbing a ridge to see what the view might be from there, or paddling at night if the moon was out. He didn't have to worry about someone else. Solitude often allows me to spend more time watching an individual bird, studying a field of flowers, or photographing the details of a landscape from multiple angles.

But solitude also gives me time to think, to go deep into my mind. In *Journal of a Solitude*, May Sarton might have captured this part best. She writes, "I am here alone for the first time in weeks, to take up my 'real' life again at last. That is what is strange—that friends, even passionate love, are not my real life unless there is time alone in which to explore and to discover what is happening or has happened." She goes on to say how much conversations with her house contribute meaningfully to her mental well-being.

Treasures from Dick's explorations of this wilderness filled the mantle: skulls, bones, rocks, and antlers. Books covered a shelf, and Dick's cooking equipment hung near the woodstove. These things would stimulate the mind, bring back memories, and create space for meditation. My finger ran across Dick's writing desk. He made it with hand

facing page |

Though not large, Dick's cabin contained all the essentials he needed to live comfortably in the wilderness.

facing page |

Dick kept detailed notes on all his adventures and projects.

tools, ripping the boards from a log, attaching the legs, and finishing the surface. He spent hours and hours sitting in front of this window, writing his journal entries, corresponding with friends, and planning his next project. What conversations did he have with himself while sitting here? I have a small table in my office that I built for my daughter when she was three. It supports a printer now, but that is not its real purpose. Every time I walk into that room, it reminds me of all the times I sat with her at that table when she was in preschool and we played teatime or had conversations with her dolls.

The mantel contains knickknacks from Dick's adventures around Twin Lakes.

The glacial blue waters of the lake lapped lazily against the shore. How often might Dick have leaned on his desk and stared out this window? Perhaps he understood the significance of his life's turn when he first stood at this window—that he was going to live in this cabin for much of the rest of his life. I put my hand on his desk, leaning forward to stare out the window, hoping no one would see my face and my teary eyes. It was slightly over fifteen years ago when I had stood at the sixth-floor window of Ann's hospital room. I'd brought her to the emergency room early the previous day, severely bloated, uncomfortable, and in pain. She had been complaining about her weight for several months but had not gone to see her doctor. Kelsie, a freshman in college, was off on a weekend trip with friends. I'd wanted to tell her that her mother was in the hospital, but Ann made me promise not to. The doctors said a diagnosis would take another two days, but she had been moved into the cancer ward. I was worried.

Ann's hospital room window framed a suburban forest of oaks, maples, and tulip trees with a few conifers that people had planted in their yards. Fresh young leaves covered the hardwoods in a wash of yellow-green hope for the coming summer. The white blossoms on the dogwoods tried to raise my spirits, even at a distance. Flowers bloomed in the beds around the hospital's parking lot, and a few American crows flew lazily across the canopy, heading north to parts unknown. Ann slept peacefully behind me as I sipped the coffee I had bought downstairs. I'd been up since first light after a restless night. Each time she moved, I would sit up, usually standing to see if she needed anything—but no, there was nothing I could do. As I watched the crows disappear to the north, I had no idea what would come.

We had been in Washington, DC, for seven years, and it had been good for all three of us. Kelsie had graduated from high school and was in her freshman year at Georgetown University. Ann was teaching at a community college, and my career was at a peak. While Ann's ovarian cancer diagnosis and treatment suspended many parts of our lives, other parts had to move forward. But, unknown to us, the direction of our lives had changed. For me, the downward slide spanned six years—slow at first and then accelerating before I hit rock bottom. For Ann, it was much quicker.

"Is that his backpack?" Dan's comment interrupted my thoughts. Hanging on the wall between the bunks was a backboard. It was flat, with shoulder straps and a little padding to rest it on his back. Dick tied everything to it. One of the home movies showed him strapping four-foot logs to it and then carrying them to his woodshed. He would tie his camera gear to it, extra clothes, food for the day, his gun, and go off for all-day hikes. He even brought back a sheep carcass and the hindquarter of a moose on that thing.

"Can we see his woodshed?" I asked the ranger. "I'd like to see the place where the weasel lived." His story of watching this weasel hunt squirrels always filled me with pure envy. We ducked low to pass through the doorway. The shed, a few dozen yards back in the woods, was still full of firewood. Dick's chopping block, where he split wood for cooking and heating, rested by the corner. Kristin dragged out his big axe, still looking as sharp as a razor. A log with a cut down from its top, stood vertically under the eaves. I leaned in close. "Do you know what that's for?" she asked. I shook my head. "It's a vice for holding his saw when he wanted to sharpen the teeth." She pulled Dick's giant crosscut saw from behind a door and proceeded to clamp it down solid. I could imagine him working each tooth with a fine file, bringing the sharpness to a peak. In the movies, I had seen him use this saw to cut firewood, rip boards, and build his house. He'd often commented about how relaxing it was to replenish the woodpile.

Far left: Dick constructed his woodshed the same way he built his cabin. Each log was carefully fitted to the next. A weasel lived there, and Dick often wrote about its daily life.

Left: Dick built this vice to hold his crosscut saw when he sharpened its teeth. His movies show him using this saw to cut all the wood for his cabin and furniture.

I asked if I could pick up the saw and the axe and feel their weight, their essence. Once in high school, I asked my dad if he wanted me to cut up a big cherry tree that had fallen in the hollow and blocked a trail. "Cut it up for firewood. It would be good to burn this winter," he said. I borrowed the pickup and the chainsaw, and filled the truck bed with a chord of wood. Then I found the double-bladed axe, the sledgehammer, and two wood wedges. I sharpened the axe the best I could, though it wouldn't have come close to Proenneke's standards. It took me several days, but I split the wood and stacked it along the side of the shed. One day a week or so later, my dad commented that the pieces might be too long to fit in the living room's fireplace. Sure enough, I had cut them all about thirty inches, and they needed to be twenty-four. We never burned any of them, and eventually the pile rotted.

Dick built this sleigh to pull behind him when he snowshoed into the wilds.

Remembering that episode brought to mind Sam Keith's comment about Dick's illness and how, after his recovery, he constantly needed to prove, at least to himself, that his body was strong again. Was my wood cutting about proving my worth to my dad? The son of a chicken farmer, I was deathly allergic to chicken feathers and eggs. A short walk into the chicken house would provoke a severe asthma attack. I had to be careful when helping bring in the hay or the dust I inhaled while stacking bales in the barn would constrict my bronchial tubes. Eating eggs caused my skin to break out in a rash that itched like crazy. I had to wear one of those big rubber masks that sealed tight against my face and featured two cloth dust filters. Some weekends, I could use it to help gather eggs. It also helped with barn work but was generally too hot and itchy for sweaty jobs. Perhaps there was more to proving oneself than I had thought.

I was the youngest of six siblings. My three oldest sisters—Kitty, Polly, and Susie—had gone off to college by the time I was born. I had two siblings still at home—my sister Barbie, three years older than I am, and my brother Wilder, eleven years older. Wilder and Barbie were athletic and strong and did well in school. My parents often told stories about how my three oldest sisters had helped bring in the hay, care for the animals, and do other chores around the farm.

My mother, Barbara, was forty-five when I was born, and my dad, George, was two years older. Both parents worked hard on the farm, and they never seemed to have problems with dust, allergies, or sweat. I, on the other hand, could barely lift a hay bale, couldn't do my fair share with the chickens, and had difficulty carrying out chores with the horses. Chicken feathers, dust, ragweed, and hay all gave me asthma. Eggs and many other foods caused me to break out in a rash. Sweat would make me itch. I have often wondered whether I developed an interest in birds because it was something I could excel at and which none of my siblings cared much about.

A distant bird call made me turn, straining to hear it again. Behind Proenneke's woodshed, a trail ran through a white spruce grove. Blueberries formed a dense understory. One spruce rose straight and tall, only eight to ten inches in diameter but probably much older than I was. It made me wonder if I was still trying to prove myself, and to whom. My parents had been dead for over forty years, and I had been a widower for more than ten. My daughter was all grown up now, living and thriving in Australia. Maybe I was more like Dick than I realized. He needed to prove to himself that he had recovered from a rheumatic fever. What was I trying to prove to myself? At sixty-seven, I could sit back and relax, but something in these wildlands still drove me.

The loud whistle of a Canada jay startled me. It came from back in the thicket behind that spruce. "Can I walk back into the woods, just for five or ten minutes?" I asked, looking at the ranger and our pilot. Dan said, "I want to go, too."

"Sure, just watch out for a black bear that has been feeding on the blueberries," she said.

"We have time," Carlon added.

Hope Creek gurgled through the trees. Dan said, "It would be nice to see the creek." Dick had often fished at the creek's mouth, catching a trout or grayling for dinner. It was the first place winter ice thawed in the spring. We zipped up the trail, continuing a conversation so as not to startle a bear. It was nice hiking with Dan. Somehow it made me think of Laurie Choate. I met Laurie through the Mountaineers a year before this trip. We got in the habit of hiking a new trail each week at Mount Rainier National Park or someplace in the Cascades. Between us, she was a stronger hiker, and I immediately began a vigorous exercise program to keep up. She had backpacked the Wonderland Trail around Mount Rainier and been to many backcountry places I'd only dreamed of visiting. Recently retired from her position as dean of nursing at a local college, she was pursuing her interest in plants and geology. Together, we refined our identification and observational skills.

The small things fascinated us, and we laughed together when we became excited by a grasshopper, the crystals in a rock, or the flight of a little blue butterfly. I had hoped she might accompany me on this trip, but it was not to be. A month after we started our weekly rambles, she was hiking with a friend on the Pacific Crest Trail when she lost her footing and fell to her death.

I asked Dan, "Do you think we should head back?" There was no sign of Dick's creek.

He nodded, and we started in that direction.

Sigurd Olson also talks about the "Great Silence" in one of his essays, referring, not to a place where there's nothing to hear, but rather to a wild place where you'll hear nothing but natural sounds: wind, water, birds, insects, and the like. It may be less about being by myself and more about being surrounded by nature. It's vital that I feel like a participant, an observer, rather than a human conqueror. Last year, when a small plane flew over my campsite deep in the wilderness of northern Washington, it was the only mechanical sound I had heard in three days; I remember how disturbing it felt.

Carlon, Mark, and the ranger had returned to the cabin and stood by the open door. I ducked inside and stood a moment, letting my eyes adjust to the subdued light. Living somewhere like this would provide the true solitude that Wendell Berry spoke about, the wild place where there would be no human obligations to impede one's

facing page |

A boreal forest surrounds Dick's cabin. The ripe blueberries are prime food for a black bear, and one had been spotted just before we started our walk.

thoughts on learning. Perhaps Berry was right. "My inner voice might become audible." But something about having a partner in one's life is even more enticing to me than solitude. Laurie would have rejoiced at experiencing all of this. I smiled while picking up the cooking spoon Dick had carved out of a piece of spruce. He sized it to ladle out one sourdough hotcake. I cooked dinner for Laurie and me on one of our camping trips—homemade chicken stew with wild rice. I learned a few weeks later that she ate mostly vegetarian food. We laughed and hugged when this came to light.

The view outside Dick's window was serene. It reminded me of the living room window in my current Seattle house. When I moved there after an unhappy five years in a noisy apartment, the change in me was instantaneous. A recurring dream I'd been having about birds, flowers, and a suburban yard prompted me to start a search for a house. On my fifth day of looking, I came across a charming place in a quiet neighborhood and went to see it the next day.

When the real estate agent opened the front door, I stepped into a living room filled with late afternoon sun. A large picture window let in loads of sunlight, causing the off-white walls and ceilings to glow with warmth. The varnished knotty pine floor sparkled. Three large rafters dropped a foot from the ceiling. They seemed like giant arms reaching out to welcome me. The white-bricked fireplace between the living and dining rooms shouted, "Come in! Stay awhile!"

I remember how I suddenly felt hopeful, and my mood, once trapped, opened its arms and stretched its legs. Within moments in that house, my mental state seemed to shift; I felt better than I had in a long time. A month later, I moved into my new home.

On my first day there, I put up a bird feeder. The next afternoon, a black-capped chickadee arrived to snatch a sunflower seed. But on the third day, a horde of birds came to my patio. Juncos and sparrows hopped around on the ground below the feeder, looking for spillage. House finches sat on the feeder, munching seeds while they looked back and forth. Black-capped and chestnut-backed chickadees zipped in, picked up a seed, and dashed away, probably going to cache them in the trees behind my place. Even a northern flicker came to the patio to check out the commotion. I had to pry myself away from the window to continue unpacking.

Anthropologist William Sax once said, "People and the places they reside are engaged in a continuing set of exchanges; they have determinate, mutual effects upon each other because they are part of a single, interactive system." A month after moving into my house, I had mostly unpacked, hung my photographs on the walls, and even hosted a dinner party for friends. I was volunteering for two outside groups and had chatted with my neighbors. Surprisingly, I felt more alive than I had in ages, less restless, no longer drifting aimlessly through space and time.

As I looked around Dick's cabin, I felt like he was standing there with me. There was so much of him in that place, and his book and videos showed how happy he was while building the cabin and

living there. Carl Jung believed that a person's house is a metaphor for their soul and mind. I've been in my house for two years, and I'm happier than I have been in a long, long time.

"We need to get back to the plane!" Mark called from outside. I listened to the wind in the trees and the water in Hope Creek. A few Canada jays called, and a raven squawked. The land here was the "Great Silence."

The view east from Dick Proenneke's cabin shows that boreal forests meet the shore of Upper Twin Lake, and tundra covers the upper parts of the surrounding mountains.

CHAPTER 8 | Building a Base

The colossal bear lumbered out of the river, right toward me. I leaned out over the railing for a better look, my hips jammed against the wooden barrier. The platform was only ten feet high, and the waters of the Brooks River lapped right up to its base. Just below me, the bear lifted his massive front foot, long black claws gleaming as the water dripped, and then put it back into the shallows. He did the same with the other leg. With four-foot-wide shoulders, he looked more like a truck than an animal. His long, dark snout pointed down, his eyes fixed to a spot a few feet in front of him. I moved my telephoto lens back and forth between his head and front feet, shutter clicking. With each step, he came closer. He must have known that all of us were there—maybe thirty people shoulder to shoulder at this viewpoint. As he strolled under the platform beneath us, his back was as big as a dining room table set for eight. If someone held my feet, they could have lowered me to run my hands through his luxurious brown coat. The bear started up a trail into dense bushes, disappeared into the shrubbery, and headed for a nap after a breakfast of salmon.

The backside of this male brown bear is the size of a small truck.

My camera went down to my chest as I watched the animal wobble through the willows. He must have stood five feet at the shoulder and probably weighed seven hundred pounds—maybe more. An Alaskan brown bear had walked under me, barely acknowledging that I existed. My hand gripped the railing and the muscles in my arms and back grew taut as my gaze returned to Brooks Falls. Another eight bears fed there, closer than the distance from home plate to center field. Five more were spread

facing page |

This big brute of a brown bear walked right under the platform where I stood, never acknowledging my existence.

throughout the river for a quarter mile below the falls. I had seen photographs of bears fishing together, but I never expected to see something like this—so much wild power right here, all controlled and focused on fish—the energy radiated out, giving the air a taste of vitality.

That bear had been enormous, and close too, but the fact that it didn't seem to notice me was humbling. I was here, part of this wild landscape, but I didn't warrant a glance from this magnificent predator. All my life, I have tried to move through nature without disturbing or altering the behaviors of a creature. So why this disquieting feeling of insignificance?

Brooks Falls at Katmai National Park is famous for viewing brown bears. They congregate at the six-foot drop where sockeye salmon must jump to reach Lake Brooks. The Park Service runs a live-stream video that allows people worldwide to watch the action, but we had come to witness it in person—to smell, see, feel, and hear what was happening. Sometimes more than two dozen bears will congregate here. Sockeye runs peak in the Brooks River in July and September, so those are the best months for bear concentrations.

I knew about the wooden platform before this trip, but I hadn't realized we'd have to walk more than a mile and a half through the forest to reach the boardwalk and the falls. From what I'd heard, the bears also often walk this path. Fortunately, the

Brown bears spread out along Brooks Falls; each has its preferred place to fish. The sockeyes congregate below the falls before attempting the leap to reach spawning areas in Brooks Lake and its tributaries.

Park Service had made the trail wide. A ten-minute safety video emphasizes the following: don't run; talk to each other, but don't shout; move at right angles off the track if you come across a bear; backpacks should contain absolutely no food, sugary drinks, or smelly stuff; never ever put a backpack down and walk away from it. After the video, the park ranger gave us a pin to indicate we had completed the safety briefing. We were to show it if stopped by another ranger. "If you wear it," he said, "the back will come off and you'll lose it."

It never occurred to me to watch the video feed before the trip. If I had, it might have given me additional insights and ideas about photographing these beasts. Somehow, experiencing Brooks Falls in person seemed much better than watching the scene on a computer screen. But I was fortunate to have the time, health, and resources to come. If we're going to protect these bears, we need more people to be aware of them, connect with them, and fall in love with the knowledge that a bear like this exists. How will they be protected from human greed and short-sightedness if they remain unknown? So, I guess the video serves a critical function.

The very first bear I saw there was not the one under the bridge. It was the one sleeping along the edge of the boardwalk that led to the overlook platform. She was lying in the bushes, only ten yards away. Her head was only partially visible, her paws pointing up and stomach bulging, her nipples in full view. She reminded me of my Jack Russell sleeping on the couch, totally relaxed and content.

My Jack Russell was trusting, unafraid of his surroundings, and not concerned that I might accidentally sit on him while he was sleeping. I told my three companions on the boardwalk that she looked like my sleeping dog. One of us could easily have thrown a spear into the exposed abdomen of the sleeping sow. Perhaps she might be more restless and less content if she knew about climate change, fishing pressures, or the possible construction of a large copper mine in this part of Alaska. Did any of the half dozen people who passed behind me while I watched this sow consider how those things might be threatening the world they had come to see?

We approached the platform overlooking Brooks Falls a hundred yards after spotting the female bear. Here, salmon are often slightly dazed after a failed attempt to climb the cascade. Nine bears were spread along the base of the falls, and one was standing at the top. They were all fishing busily. I wanted to find the bear the Park Service had named Otis. During my research for this trip, I saw photographs of Otis taken in the summer of 2014 that showed him gaining weight. Apparently, he liked to fish in the pool under the far side of the falls. Those photographs illustrated the annual challenges bears face in preparing for winter hibernation.

Otis, a large male brown bear, watches for fish in the churning waters just below Brooks Falls.

Bears can lose a quarter to a third of their body weight during their winter fast. A lactating female might burn up even more. Upon waking in spring, they feed voraciously, doing what scientists call hyperphagia. A successful bear might gain more than two pounds daily at a good fishing spot, like Brooks Falls. The photos showed Otis starting out as a lean and fit bear on July 2 and gradually gaining weight until September 22. By then, he had become round, plump, about to burst at the seams, and ready for his long winter nap.

The Park Service provided a description of Otis: his ears were set wide on his head, and his right ear flopped over. His muzzle was long, narrow, and straight. In early August, his fur was dark blond. Evidently, it darkens gradually during the summer. I used my binoculars to study each bear carefully and found one with his ear flopping over—undoubtedly Otis. He sat in the far pool, gazing down into the white, churning water, waiting for a fish. He looked like an elderly man with his elbows propped on a table, staring into his cup of coffee. Apparently, the Park Service first identified Otis in 2001. He used to fish in an area of churning water known as "the jacuzzi" out in the middle of the river; younger, more powerful males had now displaced him. According to the Park Service, he's one of the more efficient fishers and can successfully catch

salmon in September, when many others have a hard time. Evidently, he's also more tolerant of other bears than many adult males.

The word "Otis" left my lips. This name in German or English stands for prosperity, fortune, or richness. I smiled at his flopped-over ear. Otis means keen of hearing in Greek. The person beside me asked, "What?" and stepped away. The Park Service has named all these bears and produced an online guide to them. When I was in graduate school, we were repeatedly taught never to name our subjects but give them a number or letter code instead. It was thought that names might personalize the subjects and inject bias into our research. But here, names might encourage people to relate to the bears and think more about their needs and what it takes for them to survive. Our society needs more people to know and care for these animals and the wild places they inhabit. Otis plunged his head into the frothing water but came up without a fish.

Like others, Otis probably hibernates on a vegetation-covered slope more than five hundred feet above sea level somewhere in Katmai. Bears don't really hibernate, as ground squirrels do, but instead go into torpor. Their body temperature decreases only about twelve degrees, their heart rate drops to eight to ten beats per minute, and their respiration decreases to one breath per minute. Incredibly, they don't eat, drink, urinate, or defecate throughout their slumber of five to six months. Hibernating bears get enough water from their fat and are able to recycle waste to maintain their muscle and organ tissues. Perhaps some of that ability could rub off on me.

This brown bear keeps all four feet firmly on the rocks as it reaches for a jumping salmon. Sockeyes take a month or more to transition from their brown-black ocean-going color to the bright red color of breeding individuals. The fish at Brooks Falls had not yet completed their transformation.

The feeding behavior of these bears was different from what we had seen along Funnel Creek. There, they actively chased down salmon; here, it was wait and grab. One bear stood above the falls and snatched fish out of the air; others stood in pools, lunging into the water when salmon came near. Younger ones lurked downstream or along the edge, waiting for scraps to float along. Or they might sneak into a good spot while the big guy was off feasting on his catch. Some used a paw to pull salmon into their mouths or pin it to the bottom. Others stuck their heads underwater to grab a swimming fish, capturing it with their teeth.

The Park Service asked us to be quiet on the platform and not cheer when a bear caught something. Some bears are more susceptible to human disturbance than others. Evidently, a large male bear that regularly fed near the falls would immediately leave the river when a fisherman entered, even if the person was a quarter mile downstream. Over ten years, that bear never acclimated to people in the river.

The bear on the falls grabbed a fish out of the air and turned to head into the shallows. The

sockeye it clutched hadn't turned the bright red of breeding-condition individuals. It takes these fish a month or so to make the complete metamorphosis. Perhaps Brooks Falls is closer to Bristol Bay than Funnel Creek, and these salmon need more time. The carotenoids in their muscle move to their skin as they make sperm or eggs, giving them their red color. I hadn't expected to see that difference between locations—more to look up when I got back to Seattle.

Our party waits for a brown bear that has been grazing in the tundra to move out of our path.

The day before our trip to Brooks Falls, Glen took us down Funnel Creek. Along the way, he explained the rules we were to follow so that our group would not disturb the bears, who always have priority because they need access to the fish. He made us stand back in the tundra while he watched their behavior before we climbed onto a ledge where we might have a better view of the bears. This wasn't about our protection—it was about not bothering the bears. We also stayed together and were told not to create a perceived fence where the bear might want to go. Glen showed frustration when other groups failed to follow these guidelines, telling us that a Park Service ranger could write them a ticket.

Later, as I wrote about how much Glen worried that we might disturb the bears, my March 2020 trip to Mexico came to mind. There, too, paying attention to what the animals needed was far more important than getting a sighting. Off the coast of Loreto, we found six blue whales feeding in a bay an hour down the coast. At one point, our captain and head guide were clearly upset about something. As they spoke Spanish, I understood nothing, so one of my friends asked what was happening.

We counted eight boats, or pangas, on the water that day in early March. Each panga in the bay that day had four to eight clients wanting to see whales. Of course, one never knows where a whale will come up for a breath after a six- to ten-minute dive: sometimes more than a mile away, sometimes closer. Occasionally, our captain would move our panga by just puttering along slowly.

One captain, though, would move his boat at a pretty good clip, essentially chasing the breathing whale. Our guide told us that, a decade earlier, they had discovered that chasing whales by boat was disturbing the whales and making it much harder to have good sightings. The state thus instituted regulations prohibiting boat operators from racing after whales. The captains took those regulations one step further and began to self-regulate. Right after they explained this to us, we saw another boat putter over to the offender. The captain talked with him, presumably explaining that he should not pursue whales in that way. Our guide photographed the offender and said she would submit a report to the regulators. The state can and apparently does cancel permits for problem captains. Self-regulation helps maintain the locals' livelihoods.

It isn't just boats that sometimes fail to follow protocol. Along Moraine Creek in Alaska, an angler appeared mid-river and did the same thing. A large male bear wanted to move out into the creek where the man stood casting. "He's supposed to give way for the bear," Glen said. The bear paced back and forth on a sandbar a few hundred feet away. Instead of leaving, the fisherman tucked away his fishing pole, pulled out a camera, and began to stalk the bear, snapping pictures of it. The bear paced even faster, looking at the man, then away, and pacing again. Finally, it turned and ran up through the willows onto the tundra.

Glen was fuming at that point and told us about a tour company out of Homer, Alaska, that often flew in here with two Otter aircraft, each carrying ten people who wanted to see bears. But the size of the group was too much for the bears. The big male bears learned to recognize the sound of the planes and left the river, heading into the tundra, even before the people arrived. When they heard the Otters take off, the bears returned. Glen said that the customers never knew the difference, and the company no longer makes flights to Katmai. Perhaps the Park Service revoked its permit. I started to think about the consequences of such disturbances for the bears.

Salmon don't run up each creek all summer long. At Brooks Falls, summer sockeyes come in July, and fall sockeyes come in September, but there are far

An angler puts down his fishing equipment and stalks a brown bear that wants to fish on these flats.

fewer fish in June, August, or October. At Funnel and Moraine Creeks, the highest concentrations pass through in August. These are narrow windows, and the bears must maximize their feeding when the salmon run. The protein and lipids in these fish are essential to the bears as they prepare for hibernation. A successful bear might catch thirty or more fish in a day, but if people keep it out of the river for several hours, it might not be able to gain as much weight as it should. Pregnant females will abort their fetuses if they aren't in a good enough condition at hibernation. Others may have to forage longer into the fall than is preferable.

Bears, however, eat lots of things besides salmon. In the spring, they graze heavily on sedges. The new green shoots are high in nutrients. In summer, they eat grass and feast on berries. Along Funnel Creek, I saw a bear rake up blueberries with its teeth. He opened his mouth, bit into a clump of the tundra berries, and then pulled his head up, stripping the woody plant of fruit. He also spent time in a lush patch of grass and sedges, munching more like a cow than I imagined a bear might do. However, at this time of the year, salmon is what bears want most.

This bear stands to check whether several anglers have left Funnel Creek, but they continue to block its fishing interest. Tourists, including anglers, are supposed to give bears the right-of-way.

On another day, Glen made us wait forty-five minutes while a bear fished for salmon along a side stream. At the time, anglers were in the main channel, where the bear clearly wanted to fish. Each time the bear approached the main creek, he looked at those people and then went back up the side branch. When they had moved a quarter mile beyond the stream opening, the brown bear came back into the larger creek but then went up on the bank to circle the anglers and head downstream. This group had displaced the bear—he hadn't been able to live as if no people were there.

Katmai regulations say that people must keep fifty yards away from bears when fishing, and that an angler must take his line out of the water if a bear starts to approach. The trick is to get people to follow these guidelines. Glen puts the bears' needs first, but he worries that the Park Service will react to repeated bear disturbances by restricting access for everyone, and that might limit his ability to bring clients in to see the bears, even though he follows the rules and has all the Park Service permits.

Several anglers cause this bear to leave the river and walk around them. Park regulations dictate that the fishermen should give way to a bear.

Two graduate students from Kansas State University were at Moraine Creek when we walked on shore. They interviewed visitors to find out why they had come to Katmai and asked them to take an online survey. I thought they could have been more forthcoming about the study's goals. I asked if they were considering the economics of tourism. They were not, and they hadn't seemed to give thought to economics at all. Our country and society tend to overemphasize money and evaluate how we're doing based on economic growth, jobs, and making more money. Gross domestic product (GDP) is used to measure success, society's health, and our well-being. However, increasingly, people are beginning to question the legitimacy of this metric. This number includes many things that may threaten the planet's sustainability. Based on GDP, Alaska performed best the year following the *Exxon Valdez* oil spill! I was glad these researchers hadn't included economics, but I was concerned that they didn't seem to understand the issue.

Interestingly, social scientists and some economists are beginning to question the aforementioned approach and have instead been promoting the measurement of national happiness. Scientific research shows that being in a wild country supports mental health by helping people relax and recover from the stress of living in the modern world. It stimulates the human brain in positive ways. I was particularly interested in how I reacted to seeing bears, watching them fish, and being in these vast wilderness areas. I hoped that the researchers were pursuing these social questions in their study.

When I looked at the online survey later, however, I discovered that it was designed to understand a visitor's perception of their time in the back country of Katmai. We were to ignore Brooks Falls, where people come in droves. The survey used a series of photographs depicting different numbers of people to find out: first, what the visitor had hoped to experience in solitude; second, what the visitor had actually experienced; and third, what they thought managers should work toward providing. A second set of pictures depicting bears explored people's perceptions of seeing bears, the numbers seen, and their distance from the bears. The survey had no questions regarding how visitors had acted while in remote areas or how their guides handled their group's interactions with bears. I found the survey disturbing in that it hadn't asked questions about efforts being made to protect the bears or the park. It was only about visitors and how their enjoyment could be maximized.

In my ten years leading The Wilderness Society Research Department and directing the work of twelve PhD economists and ecologists and two environmental lawyers to address all kinds of wilderness issues, I spent a lot of time thinking about these questions and managing wild country. I wrote to Ryan Sharp, PhD, the professor overseeing the Kansas State University study, expressing my concern that understanding and managing the ethics of park guides and visitors was more critical than understanding people's perceptions of their experiences. It seemed to me that it would be impossible to interpret their survey results if they didn't know about the behavior of the guides and other visitors. Sharp wrote back to say that he and the managers understood my concerns but the funding for his study was restricted to the surveyed perceptions.

Asking policy-relevant questions is difficult for academically trained scientists or managers who are focused on immediate visitor use issues. When I started working for National Audubon right out of graduate school, I was asked to develop a conservation program for the threatened white-crowned pigeon, a Caribbean bird that only reaches the United States in the Florida Keys and the southern mainland. I successfully raised money and began a study of their breeding ecology. We discovered many essential and scientifically exciting things. Still, it was three or four years into the study before the relevant policy-influencing questions came to mind, things like how these birds used the suburban areas along the Florida Keys or what places were critical for the survival of newly independent young.

Answering these questions might suggest a restoration strategy for this species. A few years later, when I had obtained answers to these questions, I didn't know what to do with the knowledge or how to influence policy. Fortunately, my team partnered with the Nature Conservancy and the Florida Natural Areas Inventory to develop a detailed proposal for both state and county. I then made multiple presentations to decision-makers. The scientific reputation I had built for myself from the original work helped establish my credibility, and the policy-relevant information we provided influenced decision-makers. The state, county, and federal governments have now spent hundreds of millions of dollars protecting critical habitats, and for at least a decade, the county instituted strict building codes to protect this species' habitats.

That successful science–policy interface changed my view of science, its role in our society's perceived values, and how to implement that role. My career changed radically after that—I went from being an academic scientist to working on the science–policy interface. A few years later, I moved to Washington, DC, to lead The Wilderness Society Research Department and, maybe more importantly, help them build integrated multi-disciplinary programs that included science, policy, advocacy, and communication. We established one of those programs in Alaska, and it continues to do great things: fighting to protect the Tongass National Forest from excess logging, trying to prevent oil exploration in the Arctic National Wildlife Refuge, and developing environmentally sound management plans for the network of National Wildlife Refuges across Alaska.

The crowd around me at Brooks Falls let out a major cheer—exactly what the park ranger told us not to do—when the bear on the top of the falls chomped on a sockeye in midair. An impressive bear, her head lunged forward as she balanced on the rock edge and grabbed the fish—a very photogenic moment. I looked around at the crowded platform and thought it was more like a Disney amusement park experience than a wilderness park-preserve moment.

This young brown bear reaches out from the falls to catch a sockeye. It didn't succeed, and the fish fell back into the river to leap again.

It's critical that we figure out how to get more people to think about the needs of the bears and the wildlands we are trying to protect. How many might consider the critical nature of the relationship between salmon, bears, habitats, and the wilderness? Seeing wild animals is an early step in learning to care about them and push for their protection. Naming species and these individual bears makes the encounter with them more personal, gives them an identity, and helps acknowledge their existence among all life. I guess I did come looking for Otis. A platform like the one at Brooks Falls may be helpful, but I worry that people may not develop the sense of awe and respect that's essential for supporting conservation. They need to care for this place and its animals, and when they return home, they need to help push for policies and management plans that protect this glorious place.

Someone bumped my back as they shuffled through the crowd. There had been a constant flow of people on the platform. Some had been here as long as I; others had come and gone. The Park Service estimates that more than seven thousand people visit Brooks Falls each July, when bear viewing is at its peak. The challenge for conservation is to have more of these people develop enough caring to demand a policy agenda that will protect the bears and their resources. This wilderness needs a larger base

of support to survive. Another photographer elbowed my side hard as he shoved his way toward the railing.

Photographers are also not immune to ethical issues when interacting with wildlife. We all want that "million-dollar" shot, and some push beyond what's fair to the subject. Glen told us the story of an internationally recognized photographer who, while in Alaska, made his intern crawl through the grass toward a bear and then leap up into the air. Of course, this startled the bear, and the photographer snapped his outstanding photograph. The North American Nature Photography Association adopted the "Principles of Ethical Field Practices," which stresses that a photographer should not distress an animal or interfere with its life cycle or procurement of its needs. Glen did an excellent job of making sure our group met these criteria.

At Brooks Falls, the platform separated photographers from bears, and park volunteers in uniforms stood by to enforce rules. Right then, two bears moved out onto the top ledge—the same massive individual that had been there all day and a second, slightly smaller one. They both looked down at the cascade of water. The larger one bounced up and down on her front feet, as if calling the fish to jump. When one did jump, she moved only her head, keeping all four feet firm on the wet rocks. The younger couldn't resist reaching out with a front foot, attempting to pull the fish toward its mouth. Both leaned forward, and I wondered if they occasionally lost their balance and toppled into the pool below. They both caught fish at about the same time. The big one turned to carry its catch into the shallows while the other, closer bear returned along the falls to some dry rocks and tore its feast apart.

A brown bear plunges headfirst into the Brooks River, chasing after a large sockeye.

"We need to think about heading back," Leo said. It was mid-afternoon, and we had the walk back to the planes and then the flight to Port Alsworth. I lingered at the railing; the bears continued living their lives. Two young males had a mock fight, their mouths wide open, teeth glistening as they gnawed at each other's necks—like two puppies wrestling—and I felt blessed to watch them. Content to have some fun, they weren't in a panic about their next meal.

Bears need huge areas where they can roam and thrive. Due to their size, ferocity, and tendency to interfere with our European-based culture, they have been wiped out of most parts of their historic range in the United States and are feared by many. I once found myself three miles from the trailhead in Washington's Selkirk Mountains as the late afternoon light faded. I'd been walking through the dark woods for more than an hour to reach my car. A sign at the trailhead warned people to be aware of grizzly and black bears. Remembering my friend Nicole's comments during our canoe trip on the Kenai Peninsula, I decided I would sing. The only song I could think of was "Old McDonald Had a Farm." I started making up verses about bears after only ten minutes. It was their country, and I was happy to accommodate them.

At the bridge over the Brooks River, I stopped to scan the marsh. A female bear and two small cubs were working their way along the water's edge. Leo and Carlon, our two pilots that day, stood beside me;

they too looked out, their hands resting on the railing. I wondered how many times they had stopped to look at this scene and what they had seen, experienced, and thought while here. Coming to Brooks Falls was something I had hoped to do since I first heard of this place two decades ago.

During my graduate school studies and my work on conservation, I learned a lot about bears, predators, ecosystems, salmon, and conservation challenges. This place meant a lot more to me than just a chance to see a lot of big brown bears. It made me think of bucket lists and what I still hoped to do in my life. But there needed to be more than just checking off this or that item on a list. I wanted to experience the same stirring of emotions, the same stimulation of mind and senses that this Alaska adventure had given me.

A few hundred people looked closely at bears that day at Brooks Falls. What puzzled me as I hurried down the trail after Leo and Carlon was how we could get more people in our society to make room for these magnificent beasts in the world. Only a few people can make it here to see them in the flesh; more can see them through such instruments as live Park Service camera feeds, photographs, and stories. But we need many, many more of them to build the huge base of support needed to stop things like the Pebble Mine, the relaxation of environmental laws, or anthropogenic-induced climate change. Although they are big, strong, and ferocious, these bears need human advocates if they are to survive and thrive.

CHAPTER 9 | More than a Bucket List

A small brown bird was working through the leaf litter under the birches, probing for possible morsels. For the last ten minutes, I had been standing on my cabin's deck, looking through the trees at the bay in Port Alsworth. That morning was my last in Alaska, and soon I would be taking a plane back to Anchorage and then another to Seattle. It was just dawn, and a few ripples lapped at the shore while some small birds, probably pine siskins, chattered in the trees.

This brown bird in front of me, though—one I didn't know—drew me down onto the grass, and I drifted in its direction. It was all brownish gray on its back, wings, and tail. Darker spots dotted its off-white breasts. A thrush of some kind, and then I realized it must be a gray-cheeked thrush. I probably hadn't seen this species since high school.

Gray-cheeks are in the genus *Catharus*, which means pure and clean in Greek. The name comes from their elegant plumage. Thirteen species are recognized in this group, five migratory ones in North America and eight nightingale-thrushes, which don't migrate and live in Latin America. I had seen seven species in this genus. I began to stalk this guy.

The gray-cheeked thrush does an epic yearly migration, breeding in the taiga from Newfoundland to eastern Siberia and wintering in the northern Amazon Basin. My stalking subject flitted its wings, propelling it twenty feet across the forest floor. I knew from previous reading that this bird would start its southern migration in another month, heading across Canada and south through the eastern United States. It will possibly fly across the Gulf of Mexico to the Yucatán and then south, or it might fly directly to South America, island-hopping through the Caribbean. It will then move into the northern parts of the Amazon Basin for the winter. Next spring, it will make the trip in reverse, the same six- to seven-thousand-mile journey, and likely return to Port Alsworth to breed—breathtaking considering its size.

These thrushes weigh roughly thirty grams, less than a tenth of a pound, about the same weight as forty-eight dried garbanzo beans. Yet, it makes this trip under

| Port Alsworth is calm before dawn.

its own power, with no help from others. Its route is programmed into its brain. After laying on a substantial fat reserve, it might fly 250 miles or more in a single night. Then it refuels over a few days at a stopover point before winging another leg.

Ornithologists have designed amazing experiments to learn how birds navigate. They have raised baby birds in planetariums while manipulating the stars above them, transported birds using devices that would prevent them from detecting Earth's magnetism or the sun's direction, used mirrors to alter the sun's polarization and course, and moved adults outside their normal ranges. In doing so, they discovered that birds—including the thrushes that don't learn migration routes from their parents—have a built-in map and compass. Depending on whether they migrate during the day or night, they use a combination of the sun, the stars' rotation, Earth's magnetism, and possibly their sense of smell to orient themselves. Astonishingly, many migratory passerines return yearly to the same forest patch to breed or winter.

The gray-cheeked thrush flew up into a tree and disappeared. I thought about my flight back to Seattle, a distance much less than this bird would fly to get to its wintering grounds. I have always credited myself with a pretty good sense of direction, but there's no way I could find my way back to Seattle from here in Alaska. First, the physical requirements are far too great. I had a hard enough time hiking down to Funnel Creek and back with my camera gear. How could I possibly manage the distances and supplies needed to survive a trip to Seattle? The Klondike prospectors came by boat from the west coast to Alaska, and then went on foot. Many couldn't handle the physical demands. This bird's abilities boggled my mind, and set me to pondering how I had become so enthralled with this particular genus.

It seems funny now, but I made my first trip to Panama back in 2017 for reasons very different from the pursuit of thrushes. I flew down to meet up with a woman I'd been dating who was spending four months in Panama to study Spanish. I didn't want to go so long without seeing her, but when she said I could fly down, she had two caveats: she should not be the sole reason for my visit, and the place we met must also be fun for her.

I've always had a fascination with resplendent quetzals and three-wattled bellbirds. Through the years, I'd read a lot about these species but never seen them. Jeffrey Dietrich, owner of Mount Totumas Lodge in western Panama, told me that both species would return there by early April and there were good hiking trails through natural habitats in the vicinity.

Quetzals are revered in both Mayan and Aztec legends, and both species are important seed dispersers with interesting and different natural histories. Both are altitudinal migrants that follow the fruiting seasons of trees in the avocado family. I had read about the mutualistic relationship between these birds and plants. The trees produce a fruit high in nutrients, especially lipids, and a seed that isn't digested. The birds have an excellent source of food for raising their young, and in return, they either regurgitate or pass the seed, dispersing it around the forest.

Quetzals form pairs and work together to incubate eggs and raise young, while the male bellbirds have an interesting courtship system referred to as a lek—an aggregation of males that display in a competitive manner to attract females. Rather than assembling in one place, Dietrich said, male bellbirds spread out along a mile or more of forest at an elevation of sixty-five hundred feet, thus forming what ornithologists call a distributed lek. Females pick a male for a mate and then raise their offspring on their own.

Male quetzals have long, flowing tails, twice the length of their bodies, while male bellbirds

have a grotesquely loud call that shatters the ambience of the forest and is extremely obnoxious—like a jack-in-the-box burst. Why do these birds have a tail like that or a voice so loud? Science says it's because of sexual selection; that is, the females choose males according to these traits. The explanations make sense, but that still doesn't explain the sense of wonder they inspire

A Swainson's thrush leaps through the branches in Panama, looking for food to fuel the next leg of its migration. This subspecies winters in the Andes and breeds in Canada and east of the Cascade Mountains.

in me. I had wanted to see these species for years and ponder their evolution and legendary status.

During my Panama visit, I discovered that April is also the month when Swainson's thrushes migrate through Panama. These are common breeders in the Pacific Northwest and have an elegant song that makes them sound like a woodwind quartet. At Mount Totumas, they were practicing their melodies everywhere. This thrush winters farther south in the Andes Mountains of South America. My trip was short that year, only four days, but I also learned that another member of the *Catharus* genus lived there: the ruddy-capped nightingale-thrush, which is nonmigratory. I heard one singing, but I didn't see it.

In 2018, I returned to Mount Totumas for eight days to see if I could record the songs of the nightingale-thrush and Swainson's thrush. Apparently, ornithologists think that the genus evolved in Latin America only a few million years ago. Initially, none of the species was believed to be migratory. Evidently, the ancestor of Swainson's thrush was the first to take up this behavior. Then, the gray-cheeked line began to migrate from a separate nonmigratory ancestor. In my lifetime, DNA and mitochondria analyses have shed fascinating insight into birds' evolution.

Several theories suggest reasons for migration. Nest predation is exceptionally high in the tropics, and flying north might enable the thrushes to find areas where it is less so. Thus, the adults might be able to increase the number of fledglings. Day length is another factor; farther north during the summer, longer days give parents more time to feed their young; they might thus be able to lay more eggs in a single clutch. During spring, the northern zones also have a significant flush of insects, providing a superabundance of food for feeding hungry young. However, migration also comes at a cost. It's an energy drain, and it increases mortality rates over what resident adults might experience in the tropics. The combination of these or other factors that led some *Catharus* thrushes to migrate and others to stay put is hard to discern but intriguing to contemplate.

We often think of species as fixed and immutable during our time on Earth, but the evolution of *Catharus* thrushes is both recent and astonishing. Ornithologists believe that the gray-cheeked and Bicknell's thrushes diverged less than half a million years ago. Genetic analysis of the gray-cheeked thrush suggests that it might have survived the last Pleistocene glacial advance in a refugium near present-day Newfoundland and then rapidly spread across North America with the glacial retreat. Ornithologists think a large patch of boreal forest persisted near present-day Newfoundland, and this area, the refugium, maintained a breeding population of the gray-cheeked thrush ancestor through the height of a glacial advance. The gray-cheeked and Bicknell's ancestors apparently separated from the veery, another *Catharus,* a little less than a million years ago. Continental glaciers may have played a role in isolating their populations and allowing the separated populations to adapt to different conditions, thus becoming distinct species.

The last continental glaciers retreated and disappeared only within the last ten to twenty millennia. During that period, the gray-cheeks spread west from Newfoundland into Alaska, across the Bering Strait's land bridge, and into eastern Siberia. At the same time, humans moved east out of Siberia into Alaska and south through the Americas. Perhaps those human travelers heard and marveled at this thrush's song.

Though I have yet to hear the gray-cheeked thrush sing, the closely related veery has a beautiful song—much like an oboe's sweet notes that tumble down in pitch as the two-second melody progresses. I opened my phone and played a recording of a gray-cheeked thrush—a series of up-and-down notes—followed by an equally beautiful veery-like downward spiral. Unfortunately, no gray-cheeked thrush responded to my phone's song.

I was planning to return to Panama in the spring following my Alaska trip, to record the songs of two other nightingale-thrushes—the orange-billed, which nests at lower elevations than the ruddy-capped nightingale-thrush, and the black-billed, which nests at higher elevations. I'd seen both species on my third trip there in April 2019 but didn't have the time or opportunity to record their songs then. I was busy that year with five friends I'd brought along to share the wonder of those mountains. The black-billed nightingale-thrush lives on top of Mount Totumas, and the hike up the mountain is arduous.

Upon my return in 2020, I planned to leave equipment in place for forty-eight hours of continuous recording in hope of capturing the black-billed's melodies. I had bought new equipment and special batteries that would have allowed me to stash the gear and let it do its work. Then the coronavirus pandemic struck, and international travel was suspended.

When I grumbled to friends about my canceled trip, they asked, "Why go again? You've been there three times. Don't you want to go someplace new?" I could have planned a trip elsewhere, to a new location, but something intriguing—challenging—called me to broaden and deepen my knowledge of that place. Those mountains still pull me toward them, whispering something I can't quite make out—perhaps a detail that might help me understand my life and theirs.

After my 2019 Panama trip and six weeks before my Alaska adventure, my friend Craig Lee and I went camping in north central Washington. I hoped to record the tunes of the Swainson's and hermit thrushes. The Swainson's song is an upward-spiraling series of notes, while the hermit thrush opens with several distinctive whistles and then finishes with an elaborate flourish. The males of these two thrush species have a repertoire of six to ten songs that they use to defend their territory and attract mates. A hermit thrush serenaded Craig and me as the sun set behind Tiffany Lake. We didn't even notice the mosquitos biting and hovering about as that colorful and musical performance unfolded.

I looked at where the little thrush had flown, wishing I'd had a better look. Seeing a species like the gray-cheeked thrush stimulated thoughts about how a community of plants and animals comes about. The evolution of this genus has been influenced by ecological and geological processes occurring locally as well as continent-wide. Other species have been pressured in different ways. Species adapt, and the community in Katmai is a result of all those factors coming together. The challenge now is that humans have dramatically altered many of the pressures, making it difficult for some species to adapt and survive.

A high-pitched whistle from up the hill interrupted my thoughts. It was hard to tell, but each note seemed slightly down-slurred. On top of the knoll, I found the source. Three large finches sat in some bushes, begging incessantly. Their conical bills were robust. Their plumage was dullish brown, with maybe a tinge of yellow. They were bigger than the gray-cheeked thrush and larger than the house finches in my Seattle yard. I was puzzled at first and then recognized them as pine grosbeaks, a bird I had seen only a few times. The

female appeared a second later and fed one of the fledglings while the others continued quivering their wings and squawking.

In many respects, the pine grosbeak is the antithesis of the gray-cheeked thrush. Pine grosbeaks usually stay in Alaska all through the year. During some winters, presumably because of low food availability in their typical wintering areas, large numbers of this northern finch species fly south well outside of their normal range in what is known as a bird irruption. One of my best views of this species was in February 2012, when I found a flock feeding on aspen buds near Cle Elum, in central Washington. A foot of snow covered the ground as I hiked through a field headed toward a ponderosa pine forest. The birds were in a little ravine filled with aspens and shrubs.

Pine grosbeaks live across the taigas of North America, Europe, and Asia. They are part of the Fringillidae family—different from the thrushes. Most species in this family are either permanent residents or nomadic. My trip to Alaska has been about bears, salmon, wilderness, and mountains. Seeing the thrush and grosbeaks was an unexpected bonus; both have stimulated me to think about what drives nature and what influences it. Both species breed here in the Katmai Peninsula. But then the gray-cheeked thrushes head to South America for the winter, while the pine grosbeaks typically stay in Alaska.

The pine grosbeak, also found in northern Europe and Asia, is the only member of the genus *Pinicola*. In contrast, *Catharus* thrushes are found only in the Western Hemisphere, except for a few gray-cheeked thrush individuals that sneak across the Bering Strait to eastern Siberia. The genus *Catharus* contains thirteen species and is part of the family Turdidae. Eight of these species stay in Latin America all the time, including the nightingale-thrushes I saw. The Swainson's and gray-cheeked thrush species breed in North America and winter in Latin America. The bird families of both species are found worldwide, except in Antarctica. I recently ordered a copy of *The Largest Avian Radiation*, hoping to learn more about passerines, the order of perching birds to which these two species belong. Published in late 2020, the book is a hefty tome that sheds light on these bird groups. Undoubtedly, it will spur me to further travel.

After my Alaska adventure, I had planned a series of trips over the subsequent eighteen months to look for birds, see habitats, and explore geology and ecology: to Kenya in December, the Baja Peninsula in March, Panama in April, and Australia the following October, where I would stay for a month to visit my daughter. The COVID-19 pandemic that gripped the world made me realize how quickly plans can be upended. The Kenya and Baja trips took place, but then came March and the pandemic.

Each of my planned trips focused on specific species I hoped to find and geologic or ecological features I wanted to explore. The pandemic not only halted travel for my individual type of scientific exploration, it also halted larger-scale scientific research on birds and ecosystems. The lodge owner at Mount Totumas told me that a group of entomologists that visited his place every summer to study insects had to suspend their work because of COVID-19. Similarly, biological stations such as the one on Barro Colorado Island in Panama were closed. Fieldwork was entirely suspended.

Thoughts of thrushes, grosbeaks, birds in general, and other places I had visited rushed through my mind, even while I was in Alaska and totally absorbed by my surroundings. "Everything is connected," sounds like a cliché, but it's very true in many interesting ways. Katmai is unique on many levels, but it's also a product of geologic and ecological processes taking place on a global scale. The gray-cheeked thrushes are here due to certain factors that drove the evolution of the genus, including the Pleistocene glaciation. Maybe something else allowed the evolution and spread of pine grosbeaks. The brown bears had been an incredible thrill to see on this trip. The last glaciation is thought to have played a role in separating their ancestral populations. Those among them who were isolated north of the continental ice sheets evolved into the polar bear, while those who were isolated south of the continental glacial ice became the grizzly—or brown—bear that I saw.

Seeing a new species stimulates a robust curiosity in me. I want to understand how these creatures make a living, how they evolved, and how they formed relationships with other species and the environment. After trips, I often follow up, trying to determine whether science has answered some of my questions. After my 2018 Panama trip, my readings fed my fascination with the genus *Catharus*.

My trip plans always include looking for specific plant and animal species. On my 2016 trip to the Cape York Peninsula in Australia, I told my guide that I wanted to see an epiphyte called the ant plant and a long-necked turtle. This plant has what is called a mutualistic relationship with an ant, a bird, and a moth—the four species work together to increase their chances of survival. The long-necked turtle, a primitive member of the order Testudines, can't withdraw its head into its shell, unlike all the other turtles I've seen in North America. My guide gladly found the ant plant for me but refused to look for the turtle because it would put us at risk of an estuarine crocodile attack. My knowledge about that species has thus remained confined to what I learned about it in graduate school forty years ago. My travels are about more than adding a species to my life list or ticking off a destination on a bucket list. The trip to Alaska, like these others, has been about watching, observing, listening, and recording what I see, and thinking about the world and how it behaves. Maybe I should have taken that university position.

facing page |

A black-billed nightingale-thrush jumps through the cloud forest of Panama. This species is in the genus *Catharus*, a close relative of the gray-cheeked and Swainson's thrushes. My curiosity about this genus encouraged me to look for this species on a trip to Panama.

CHAPTER 10 | "You Ready?"

"Okay, the pilot wants you to board," the young man said. He had just walked into the hangar where we were waiting—the six in my group and another couple. We were headed to Anchorage and then home after spending five days in the Alaskan outback. Our luggage had already been stowed.

We shuffled out the door and around the tail of the King Air, a two-propeller plane sitting beside the dirt runway in Port Alsworth. I was second in line as we approached the foldout stairs near the back of the fuselage. At least five seats ran up each side of the dark interior. No one was sitting in the copilot seat, so I scrambled into a seat right behind it, careful not to hit my head on the ceiling.

"Can someone ride up here with you?" I asked the pilot, referring to the copilot seat. The pilot had his green headset over his ears and the mic pulled up as he checked all the instruments on the dashboard. The windows in the front would be much better for aerial photography. Besides, I was hoping that Glen Alsworth Sr. would be our pilot and that I could chat with him. I had ridden in the copilot seat from Anchorage to Port Alsworth a week ago and enjoyed our conversation.

The pilot said, "Yes, someone can," as he waved his hand around and then looked up at me. It was indeed Glen. He flashed a broad smile and said, "Have you run out of film yet?" His gray beard and white hair looked recently trimmed. At sixty-five,

he was still in top shape—more like a caribou buck than an overweight beagle like me.

He had teased me on the way over from Anchorage and asked, "How many pictures will you take?" I'd crawled over the foredeck and slipped in beside him, trying not to touch the yoke or pedals, and replied, "Maybe ten thousand." I doubted I would actually shoot that many, and I wondered why I settled on that number. He had quite a laugh at that, though, and asked me what I would do with all those images and how the dickens I would ever go through them. I had no idea. Now, I was too embarrassed to tell him that, as it turned out, I had already topped eleven thousand and was expecting to take more pictures on the flight back. Glen Sr. had been in the Farm Lodge dining area for an Alsworth family dinner the previous evening. Ten of them, representing four generations, gathered around one of the four large tables. Glen recognized me, introduced me to his wife Patty, and asked me where my camera was. I'd laughed.

Now, I settled into my seat in the King Air, fastened my shoulder harness and seatbelt, and put on the headset. Glen was busy exchanging hand signals with the ground crew and talking to the flight coordinator at Port Alsworth. When the thumbs-up was signaled, he started up both engines and taxied out onto the runway, turning to head southwest. I held my camera above my head, pointing down the track, movie mode running. Brakes on, Glen revved

facing page |

Two young brown bears wrestle during a pause from fishing for salmon below Brooks Falls.

143

the propellers and released the restraint. We shot down the runway, accelerated, lifted off, and then banked to the right over Lake Clark. It was a smooth takeoff, even with the massive cloud of dust that shot out behind the wings.

The plane climbed gradually. It was twenty miles to the northeastern end of Lake Clark and an hour's flight to Anchorage. Pointing at a small grass airstrip on the north shore, I said, "We flew over Governor Hammond's place yesterday." Hammond was the fifth governor of Alaska, serving from 1974 to 1982—critical years in the conservation of Alaska's wild country. He died in 2005.

There was a long pause, and I worried that I had said something wrong. Glen's hands came off the steering yoke as he turned to look at me, a sheen in his eye. "The governor was a good friend of mine and a good politician. He was a representative in the legislature or maybe a senator at the time," he said, his hands waving to indicate that his exact position at the time really didn't matter for the story. He told me that the federal government needed Alaska to pass a bill that would authorize the state to manage its wildlife and fish. It was a must-pass bill, but it was dead on arrival in the legislature; at that time, the state voted down anything the feds wanted.

Alaska became a state in 1959, and Hammond was in the state legislature for much of the 1960s. Glen continued, "Jay asked the speaker to let him write the preamble to the bill." It was eloquent and flowery, covering all the great things about Alaska, but crucial to his strategy, it was written in such a way that a "yes" vote would really be a "no" vote. If a representative voted "no" on the bill, he would actually be voting in favor of Alaska taking on the management of its fish and wildlife—just what the federal government needed.

Glen looked at me throughout this conversation, making me wonder who was flying the plane. He said that one of the representatives tried to ask the speaker a question when the bill came up for a vote, and the speaker cut the man short, dismissing his question and commenting about the bill having been composed in Hammond's writing style.

Lake Clark extends east into the mountains. A significant geologic fault runs under the lake and helps form this water body.

Apparently, another critical part of their strategy lay in how Hammond and the speaker planned to use the legislature's giant electronic vote recording board. It displayed each member's vote as it was cast. When the voting started, both Hammond and the speaker quickly cast "yes" votes. The other members knew the two wanted the bill to pass, so they all voted the opposite way. Glen's hands returned to the yoke and he turned to face forward again as he chucked and finished his story—Hammond and the speaker got the vote they needed, and the state manages its fish and wildlife to this day.

The plane gained altitude as it approached the end of Lake Clark. A valley weaves from the lake up to a low pass and then down to Cook Inlet. I had hoped we might fly through the pass. It had been full of fog on our way over, so we went high above the mountains. The valley and pass run along Lake Clark Fault, an active seismic area. The Aleutian Range is pressing against the Alaska Range as the underlying Pacific and North American Plates collide. The movement is rapid by geologic standards, seven centimeters a year. The fault and its current displacement of almost eight miles helps form Lake Clark, which is over a thousand feet deep.

"Are we going to fly through the pass?" I craned my head forward to see where we were headed.

"No. It would be too rough. We'll climb to seven thousand feet and go above the mountains," he said as he glanced out the other window.

"Too much turbulence today?"

"No. Turbulence comes in the afternoon, when the sun heats the earth. The chop now is from the eddies formed from the prevailing winds." He pointed out the plane's left side and up through the mountains. I knew that these winds came primarily from the northeast at this time of the year, but I had yet to think about the eddies and backwashes they might create. I pressed my face to the window to look straight down at the last of the valley.

There was a pause. Glen was focused on adjusting instruments on the dash, not looking out the windshield. A big color screen, maybe six inches high and four inches wide, showed a map of Lake Clark and the approaching mountains. A straight red line, maybe our course, ran across the display. Perhaps that symbol on the screen was our aircraft.

He raised his left hand and waved it in a circle. "It's a little more humid in August, and the fires up north have calmed down. We had a lot of smoke in June and July, making visibility poor. Now, it's the humidity and a little smoke that are making it worse." The mountains had a distinctive gray haze across them. A satellite photograph from mid-July showed a massive swath of smoke flowing counterclockwise from southeast Alaska through the central part of the state and then down over the Katmai Peninsula before swinging up toward the Bering Strait. Alaska had record heat this summer, and with it came massive wildfires. By

facing page |

The North Fork Big River runs east from Lake Clark Pass to Cook Inlet in Alaska. The Lake Clark Fault underlies this valley and Lake Clark itself. The fault, 225 kilometers long, separates the Alaska Range and the Chigmit Mountains.

late July, more than two million acres had burned. Whether people believe it or not, climate change is affecting Alaska.

Out both sides of the plane stretched Lake Clark National Park. This park is as big as Katmai National Park. Nothing in the lower forty-eight states approaches the size of these protected areas. In 1980, the park and preserve were formalized when Congress passed the Alaska National Interest Lands Conservation Act (ANILCA) and President Jimmy Carter signed it. The park protects many spawning areas of the largest sockeye salmon run in the world. It has international significance for its wildlife, subsistence, and historic values, which are recognized in its charter. The park's purpose is "to protect a region of dynamic geologic and ecological processes that create scenic mountain landscapes, unaltered watersheds supporting Bristol Bay red salmon, and habitats for wilderness dependent populations of fish and wildlife, vital to ten thousand years of human history."

Glen brought my attention back. "That's Mount Iliamna to our south. It has been dormant for recorded history," he said, his hand extending in front of me. The volcano, ten thousand feet high, rose above the snowcapped mountains. The haze made its outline hard to see, but the cone appeared remarkably symmetrical. The top sits at the northern end of a three-mile-long ridge that's part of the original volcano. Time has significantly eroded it. Perhaps it was once much higher. A massive landslide near the summit had occurred the previous June. The interaction between ice and active fumaroles contributes to the volcano's instability. Geologists consider it one of the twenty most hazardous volcanoes in the United States.

facing page |

The mountains of the Alaska and Aleutian Ranges are rugged, snow-covered, and wild. Most of Lake Clark National Park is a designated part of the National Wilderness Preservation System.

I couldn't help myself—I went back to thinking about all the wild landscape in Alaska and how much this land meant to me, even though I had spent much of my professional life working on conserving other places. When Alaska became a state in 1959, the federal government gave it the right to select 105 million acres of public land for its use. The oil-rich area around Prudhoe Bay was part of that claim, but before the trans-Alaskan pipeline could be built, the state and federal governments needed to settle the Native peoples' land claims. To pave the way for the pipeline, Congress passed the Alaska Native Claims Settlement Act in 1971. The legislation provided forty-four million acres of land and nearly a billion dollars to Native corporations and extinguished any other claims to Aboriginal lands in Alaska. However, it failed to resolve the rights of Natives to access resources for subsistence, nor did it deal with the conservation of public lands, those owned by all Americans. Congress authorized the secretary of the interior to withdraw eighty million acres from development. These were to be studied for possible designation as national parks, national wildlife refuges, national forests, wild and scenic rivers, and wilderness, but these withdrawals were not permanent.

A pillar of steam rises from Mount Redoubt in the Chigmits portion of the Aleutian Range. This stratovolcano last erupted in 2009.

Mount Redoubt was visible on the right side of the plane. We would pass north of it and have a good view, even with the haze. I pointed out, "We flew around that yesterday. Carlon did a nice job of letting all of us see the top." Carlon had been our pilot in the Cessna that took us out of Port Alsworth to observe glaciers and this particular volcano. The steam rising from its crater was visible even in the King Air, and a few clouds clung to the top ridges.

"Could you see the large mound of lava?" Glen asked. A dome a few hundred feet tall had formed in the middle of the crater, which was blown out on the northwest side. Steam rose from all over the black mass. "It seems to go off about every twenty years. The last time was in 2009," he continued. I remembered hearing that the ash plume it sent out had shut down the Anchorage Airport and disrupted air traffic. Glen looked at me with a stern facial expression. "It doesn't get the credit it deserves. I think its eruptions have been bigger than Mount St. Helens, but no one was killed, and no one lives near it, so no one pays attention."

In front of us, a large snowfield covered much of a flattish mountain top. I pointed through the

Snowfields at the top of Double Glacier Mountain feed the ice river. Here, snow gradually builds up and compresses to ice, then flows down the mountain.

windshield. "Those snowfields are impressive, with the glaciers coming off them from several sides." I stretched my body high so I could photograph the massive snowfield. I had seen it yesterday from a lower altitude.

"We call that Double Glacier," Glen said. "See how the two glaciers come off from it and curl down the mountain."

"Yesterday, Carlon flew up one of the glaciers,

The black lines are the rocks and dirt pulled along by the glacier. Each bar represents the junction between two glaciers that came out of separate valleys and joined to form one.

just a few hundred feet above it, giving me a fantastic view," I said as I stretched to one side for another glimpse of the distinctive black lines that marked where different ice flows had come together. They reminded me of the yellow caution lines painted on roads.

"The snow on the top is still pretty good," he continued. The top was pure white. "As the summer progresses, the melt will eventually expose the ash laid down from the last eruption of Redoubt. Then the melt will speed up." Dark colors absorb more of the sun's energy. It's a recurring theme across the Arctic. Snow and ice reflect most of the sun's energy, while the darker colors of water and ground tend to absorb it. Ground or water heats faster than snow or ice, increasing the warming and thus the melting.

The national park's wildlands stretched out in every direction. Glen saw me looking back and forth. "It's rugged down there, hard to get around. That's Spurr in the distance." The northernmost volcano in North America was barely visible through the dense haze. I was thinking about how close we had come to losing all of this. During the Carter administration, the withdrawals allowed by the Alaska Native Claims Settlement Act were about to expire, reopening a vast swath of lands for exploitation. Legislation was introduced in Congress in 1977 to protect this region and provide subsistence access for Native peoples, but it didn't go anywhere.

Late in 1978, after Congress failed to act, President Jimmy Carter and Secretary of the Interior Cecil Andrus used the Antiquities Act to withdraw and protect 150 million acres. The initial boundaries for Lake Clark National Park were laid out then. An uproar resulted. Cries of "federal land grab" were common, but those doing the shouting failed to recognize that these lands belonged to all Americans, not just to those who wanted to exploit them or who lived in Alaska.

Jay Hammond was integral to all these discussions. An influential conservationist, he worked hard to protect the Bristol Bay salmon fisheries and the wilds of Alaska. As governor, he

Glaciers cover the tops of the Aleutian Range in Alaska. A large snowfield comes from the lower right and feeds the glacier headed downhill. The lines in the ice show how the ice has moved and been compressed between the valley walls. Mount Redoubt lies in the distance.

made numerous trips back and forth to Washington, DC, oftentimes to deal with these issues.

Earlier, Glen had told me a funny story about Governor Hammond. Once, when his plane was delayed from DC, they held his connecting flight in Chicago. His state trooper bodyguard had to wear a suit, but Hammond always dressed in jeans and a flannel shirt. The airline told all the passengers they were holding the plane for the governor of Alaska. According to Glen, no one likes politicians, and now, this guy was delaying their flight. The glares were intense when the governor and his bodyguard stepped into the plane. Hammond is said to have looked at his bodyguard and said, "Well, Governor, I'm going to sit here." Everyone then glowered at his suit-clad companion.

President Carter's actions spurred Congress to work seriously on a bill and pass it before he left office. On December 2, 1980, the president signed the Alaska National Interest Lands Conservation Act (ANILCA), which protected more than 104 million acres in thirteen national parks, sixteen national wildlife refuges, two national forests, two conservation areas, and twenty-six wild and scenic rivers. Wilderness designation, our highest level of protection, overlaid fifty-seven million acres of public land. ANILCA was clearly one of the most critical conservation actions taken in this country. I would put that law in the same category as the Endangered Species Act, the Clean Air Act, and the Clean Water Act—laws that make life in America better for all people.

Had President Reagan been in office earlier, along with his Interior secretary, James Watt, we would never have protected any of this land. So much of America might have been lost to greed. We are lucky to have had leaders like Carter, Andrus, and Hammond, who were committed to protecting these treasures.

A statement of Theodore Roosevelt's comes to mind: "Here is your country. Cherish these natural wonders. Do not let selfish men and greedy interests skin your country of its beauty, its riches, or its romance." Vigilance is still required to protect these lands because developments such as the proposed Pebble Mine are not reversible.

In 2018, Congress passed legislation officially naming the designated wilderness in Lake Clark National Park the Jay S. Hammond Wilderness Area. Hammond believed in keeping wild countries wild. He and his wife Bella had worked closely with the Park Service to help establish protections. Later, I wished I had asked Glen Sr. what his thoughts were about ANILCA and Hammond's role in its passage. Glen's family business is linked to taking people into lands protected by that law. His father, though, had homesteaded Port Alsworth. I would guess Glen Sr. had mixed emotions that might have changed over time.

As we flew over this national park, my concern about whether I had accomplished enough in my career filled me with dread. My goal in graduate school was to become a university professor and study birds, but I passed up a position at Ohio State University to go to Washington, DC, and work on the science–policy interface for The Wilderness Society. I regret not writing more scientific papers on my Florida research. I'd always planned to but never had the time for it.

Perhaps I could also have done more to push for helpful legislation in DC or influence federal agencies. It requires a unique approach to influence the thinking of policy- and decision-makers—one that uses science but also speaks to values. Had I known then what I know now, we might have done a better job of protecting the environment. Maybe, if I had written more for a broader audience or written more op-eds, I might have helped broaden support for environmental protections.

Many scientists think that their role is to do the science and it's someone else's job to show the public what it means and work to influence policy. They worry that their credibility as scientists will be hurt if they spend time on policy issues. What's more, university systems don't reward scientists for working on policy issues and educating people on the consequences of laws and regulations or of relaxing laws and regulations. Tenure is achieved by publishing in peer-reviewed journals, and a young professor is often penalized for engaging in policy. I passed up doing more original research to be an interpreter, an influencer—a rainmaker. The wilds need more scientists in policy fights.

I stretched as high as possible to look out Glen's side window. The plane flew above seven thousand feet, and a deep valley with a free-flowing river ran toward Cook Inlet and back behind us into the mountains. We had passed over the divide, and I asked Glen if he sometimes flew up this valley. He pointed at the color map on his dashboard. "Yes, we fly right along this and then over the pass and down into Lake Clark. It's rough going, though." The saddle between the drainages is about one thousand feet, and the mountains rise a long way up both sides. It looks like a maze. He continued, "When the clouds are thick, that can be the only way to get through. I slow down the plane as much as possible, like when you're driving over a speed bump with your car." I figured the plane would be jostled quite a bit going through the valley.

facing page |

Nooks and crannies throughout the Alaska and Aleutian Ranges hold permanent snowfields that feed glaciers. Cook Inlet borders the east side of these mountains and Lake Clark National Park.

As the plane slid out over Cook Inlet, Glen's navigation system indicated we were only nine minutes away from Merrill Field. The tide was out, and extensive mudflats spread out to the north. Our altitude dropped to a thousand feet. Glen pointed across in front of me. "See those harbor seals, maybe forty or fifty up on that sandbar?" He dipped the wing so I could photograph them.

As we approached the airfield from Cook Inlet, Glen began his conversation with ground control, and I reflected on the week I had spent in this spectacular country. It was wild and truly untrammeled by humans. The two national parks and the area between them stretched over an area close to the size of New England, yet only a few thousand people lived there. The landscape still contained all the large mammals that were here when Europeans arrived. In the lower forty-eight states, only the Yellowstone region can claim that, because humans have allowed wolves to repopulate the park.

The Florida Everglades seemed vast when I worked there, but Everglades National Park is only a fraction of the size of one of these parks. When I flew over it in small planes or went by boat to study birds in remote places, I thought the Everglades immense. Even with its huge size, the entire ecology of the marshland has been transformed because of altered water flows. Humans drained over half the marsh and altered the timing, quality, and volume of water coming through the rest. Our work led me into restoration planning. I served on several committees at work on those plans and then collaborated with lawyers in crafting legislation. Thinking of Aldo Leopold, I surmised that humans had failed to "keep all the parts of the wheel" in the Everglades. The effort to restore this magnificent wetland and protect its wildlife continues.

However, all the pieces and species are still present in Alaska's Katmai Peninsula. One might think that protecting four million acres in one of these parks would be sufficient, but the brown bears, the people, and the ecosystem need salmon to prosper and survive. The salmon need streams filled with clean, cool water to spawn and live for their first few years. They then grow by feeding on the resources of the North Pacific before returning to Alaska to reproduce.

The people of Alaska and America thought that the waters of Katmai would be protected when the EPA denied the Pebble Mine permit. Science clearly showed the adverse effects that this mine would bring, but the Trump administration immediately reversed the decision and started a fast-track permitting process. After the mine's owner visited the EPA administrator, the EPA decision was voided. The arrogance of ignoring the EPA's professional staff, the scientific analyses, and the probable effects of the mine operation on the ecosystem, salmon, and people is staggering. The "greed" President Roosevelt referred to had come back to "skin" us. The long fight to guard these waters must continue. The battle to protect natural places seems never-ending, but once they're lost, they're gone forever.

Consider the insidious effects of climate change on the viability of the Alaska wilderness. The warming of freshwater may decrease the reproductive success of salmon and affect their survival. Several years ago, I listened to a report on the results of a frightening study conducted in the Yukon. The warming temperatures stimulated parasite growth in adult salmon, causing the fish to weaken during migration, and fewer were reaching breeding areas. Historically, salmon had these parasites, but they became fatal only when water temperatures began to rise. In the North Pacific, acidification and warming also decrease salmon's food supply, slowing their growth and reducing their chances of survival.

Our society's hubris toward this threat is mind-boggling. Climate change is real and needs to be addressed if we hope to maintain something like what we have now. The wildness here is breathtaking, and the opportunity for solitude is immense. Wilderness designation, however, is not enough. Here in Alaska, these parks and state lands are vast, but the likes of a Pebble Mine, alterations from climate change, or a slip in the management of the salmon harvest could destroy this treasure.

On my Alaska trip, I saw land that still functioned much like it did before Europeans arrived in North America. I also saw parts of a state that lie at the center of a controversy around what values should drive our nation's policies. Should it be our priority to protect a sustainable environment that supports Aboriginal cultures, fishing, tourism, hunting, and our reverence for the existence of these awe-inspiring places, or should the capitalistic greed of exploitation by distant people and corporations drive their destruction? It seems the world is at a turning point. Do we knuckle down, abandon the culture of exploitation that arose in the Little Ice Age, and focus on sustaining the world and its people, or do we continue to degrade our planet?

As our return flight to Anchorage neared its end, I looked back over my shoulder toward the Katmai Peninsula and realized it had been six years since I left a salaried job in conservation. Science and conservation had shaped my identity, but they now seemed gone from my life. At times, the regret of not doing more and no longer being in the same kind of fight has been strong. Staring back into the plane's cabin, I realized, though, that a new calling had consumed me—a desire to help people experience the wilds, see things they might otherwise miss, and experience a sense of wonder and awe in nature. Over the next few months after my Alaska excursion, I would be leading a series of field trips, teaching a birding class, undertaking some writing assignments, and delivering several presentations. I have taken on volunteer leadership or science advisory roles in several nonprofits. My time is even more committed than when I was being paid.

Staring across Cook Inlet, I realized how much this trip had fed my passion for the wilderness and allowed me to feel that I was just a minuscule part of nature, a speck in the fabric of life and time. But it also reminded me of the importance of companionship, of friends with whom to share the glorious wonders of our planet. This primeval wild country had engendered a stronger sense of awe within me than I'd expected to experience. Something about seeing brown bears up close, behaving as brown bears should, invigorated my soul.

Just then, Glen Sr. looked over at me and asked, "You ready?" He had started the final approach to the runway in Anchorage. I nodded, thinking that the fight to protect this wild country would continue. Perhaps we can somehow find the humility to give this land the respect it deserves. Its salmon, bears, caribou, tundra, mountains, people, and cultures remain crown jewels of America that we must cherish and preserve.

facing page |

The creeks, wetlands, tundra, and forests of the Katmai Peninsula support a complex food web. Protecting the integrity of this ecosystem requires a comprehensive conservation strategy that extends well beyond the peninsula's borders.

CHAPTER 11 | Metamorphosis

Seattle seems quiet on this September day. A black-headed grosbeak is feeding on sunflower seeds, and a few juncos are hopping around the ground under my feeders. Smoke from wildfires in Washington, Oregon, and California fills the air with a thick, acrid haze. Consequently, no one is out in their yards or on the street. In the past many months, the coronavirus has spread worldwide, and my travel sphere has been reduced to this neighborhood and outings for groceries and exercise. Still embedded in my mind, though, is Alaska and the trip I took there some thirteen months ago. I sit on my patio with these few birds, trying to understand that trip and what it meant to me.

The grosbeak in my Washington yard makes me think of the caribou on my Alaska trip. This bird is about to migrate south to spend the winter in Latin America. Caribou are also migratory, traveling between summering grounds on tundra and wintering grounds in boreal forests. I searched for these magnificent mammals daily and spotted many caribou trails from the plane as we flew low over the rolling plains. Their paths were everywhere, forming parallel and crisscrossing lines that zigged and zagged. When I asked Glen Jr., our guide, about finding some caribou, he said I should come back in September and he would fly me to the caribou. He had a plane with big tires that could land on the tundra.

Finally, on the afternoon of our fourth day, we found some. We were lucky because the Park Service said caribou routes in Katmai National Park are generally far from where people go to look for bears. We were hiking back to the float-planes from where we had been photographing bears feeding on sockeyes. A large pair of antlers stuck above the tundra and made me stop. Only the bull's two ears and parts of its eyes showed. The caribou was in a dip behind a rise, maybe a quarter mile south of Funnel Creek. I hoped he would step onto the high ground so I could have a look at him, but he dropped backward, disappearing into the hollow. Quickly, I scanned the tundra; caribou usually live in herds.

Caribou migration is legendary. The porcupine caribou herd might be the most famous because of the continued controversy over efforts to open the Arctic National Wildlife Refuge to oil and gas development. The porcupine herd winters in forests south of the Brooks Range. The Gwitch'in people, who live south of the mountains, depend on these animals for a significant part of their subsistence. In the spring, the caribou begin a thousand-mile journey to their calving grounds on the refuge's North Slope. They must cross dangerous rivers swollen with snowmelt, traverse mountain passes, escape predators, and reach the plains before giving birth. There, the hordes of mosquitos and biting flies harass them constantly,

facing page |

A black-headed grosbeak pauses on the fence before it dashes into the neighbor's yard. This migrant heads to Latin America for the winter and returns to North America the following spring.

163

keeping them moving. The journey is momentous and arduous, and the Gwitch'in consider the North Slope sacred because it helps sustain the herd and, therefore, their culture.

Along Funnel Creek, a young buck and several cows trotted out of the ravine and toward the far slope. Their gait was more like a prance—bouncy, fluid, and spellbinding. Alaska is home

A caribou looks across the tundra toward where we stand watching. Both male and female caribou have antlers.

to thirty-two caribou herds made up of about three-quarters of a million individuals. More than half live in the western Arctic. The ones that ran in front of me were part of a smaller herd on the west side of the Alaska and Aleutian Ranges. These ungulates can run up to fifty miles a day. Their persistence is admirable, incredible, and enviable.

Caribou endurance is legendary and revered by Native Alaskans. During migration, these animals constantly move. My trip to Alaska, in many respects, was the end of an endurance run that began after I moved to Seattle from the East Coast. Sitting on my patio after the Alaska trip, I began to realize how pivotal my Katmai excursion had been for my inner self. It had allowed me to become embedded in the wilds—in nature unfettered—and absorb its wonders and gifts. It also allowed me to reflect on my life and appreciate the progress I had made since Ann's death and the implosion of the organization that was my last employer. The wilds of Alaska had been the critical medicine I needed to complete my climb out of the pit of despair.

Nature is powerful if one gives it a chance. Florence Williams summarized the science behind how nature helps us in her book *Nature's Fix*. Being in nature allows us to relax, reducing the stress running through us and making us more aware of our surroundings. The wild has a beautiful way of helping us deal with life's stresses. I've noticed that since COVID-19 struck, my time on my

patio with the birds or my short walks at a local park have made me feel calmer and better able to face the day. I've typically been more productive around my home after spending time with nature.

As I now think about it, that has always been the case. It was my time out on the farm during my childhood or weekend walks while working in Washington, DC, that helped most. The value of nature was particularly telling on a weekend soon after 9/11. I had become unpleasant around the house, short-tempered, unhappy. Ann and Kelsie had left for an outing and I went to a local park, taking my camera along. The fall colors, the reflections on the ponds, and the patterns of the trees did their trick. My time in the midst of nature strengthened me and made life bearable, helping me prepare for the coming week. My family noticed the change when they walked through the door later that day. I was reading on the couch, and apparently, my posture showed that I had relaxed.

Caribou are also respected for their strength. Their long, skinny legs don't give these animals the appearance that they can cover great distances. The tundra is often soft and muddy at stream crossings, and then there are the ups and downs of the rolling terrain. The three caribou I saw had skipped across the distant tundra with no evidence of stress, looking as if they were limber and full of energy. I chuckled to myself while sitting on my patio. I wished I could have channeled some of their strength when I was in Alaska. Strength, though, seems to be about more than just muscle; it's also about standing up to things and adjusting to change. The memory of that sorrow pit was fading as I undertook the Alaskan trip. With the onset of COVID-19, we now needed new strength and the ability to make some adjustments in our way of life.

I agreed to teach a beginning birding course in May 2020, at the height of COVID-19. We offered it over Zoom, and the response was overwhelming. More than 180 people joined the class. Everyone was hungry for nature. For me, one of the most rewarding parts of that experience came at the end of the course in a comment I received from a participant. During the course, I encouraged students to work on learning fifteen bird songs—no more. I provided them with the songs of species I thought they were likely to hear when they walked around their neighborhood. In the last class, one person was bubbling with joy, telling me about all the birds she was now hearing around her house. She hadn't realized how much life was present there.

In the first eight months after the start of the COVID-19 pandemic, I stopped leading hikes, teaching in-person classes, and having people in my house. I canceled foreign trips and didn't plan any faraway adventures, although I did buy tickets for a mid-2021 performance of *Hamilton* in Sydney, Australia. Perhaps I could visit Kelsie if travel opened back up. She's not optimistic that Australia will let Americans in before the effectiveness of a vaccine is proven and the whole world has been immunized.

The absence of future plans has been challenging, and having this possible trip on the horizon gives me a ray of hope. Many things are still doable, however: birding, hiking, working around the house, cooking, and occasional walks with close friends. I've shifted my teaching to online and am taking a course to learn how to use new tools that will improve my classes. It's both challenging and exciting. My focus is now on helping others see nature in new ways and learn to identify organisms; it's also about encouraging people to appreciate animals and plants. This is an invigorating new challenge.

I remember the incredible energy that surged through me at one point in Alaska. We had been watching the caribou for five minutes before I realized that a mile or more away, on the far hill, at least a dozen of these animals were dashing up the steep slope. They ran smoothly, occasionally stopped to nibble on vegetation but generally persisted in their goal of gaining the hilltop and disappearing out of our sight.

Caribou are spiritual animals for many because of their ability to survive Alaska's harsh climate. In simple terms, their ability to run up that hill as if it were level ground showed all the qualities that people revere: endurance, strength, and perseverance. They were a long way off, and my party became bored and began to continue along the creek, but I stood watch-ing. Finally, I had to follow, but I kept my eyes on the caribou. There was something about them that captured my soul; and now, sitting in Seattle a little over a year later, they've captured my imagination again.

A small herd of caribou works it way along the tundra near Funnel Creek. These caribou migrate annually between summer feeding grounds on the tundra and wintering areas in the boreal forests.

Alaska holds a special place in the hearts of many Americans, including mine. It's still wild, and that gives it a mystic aura. It has bears, wolves, caribou, moose, salmon, and so much more. The immensity of the places therein and the distances between them make Alaska hard to comprehend. I can't help but feel a spiritual connection to it, even though I was trained as a scientist and practiced science throughout my paid career. Sticking to just the facts is critical in the research, policy, and management arenas. Bringing in the less tangible things, such as how nature makes one feel, is thought to reduce a scientist's credibility. Yet, there has always been something intangible about being in nature and watching other living things move forward with their lives. Perhaps I learned this from my mother, who always showed reverence for life and wild things.

Thinking of my mother reminded me of the female brown bear and two cubs we had seen earlier on the day we spotted the caribou. Our guide had taken us a half mile below the falls on Funnel Creek. He thought it might afford us some views of different bears. Not long after we settled on the southern cliff above the river, someone spotted a female brown bear and her cubs moseying along the far ridge, coming right toward us. The bear dropped over the edge and worked down a steep two-hundred-foot slope to the water. Her cubs were comical, slipping and sliding down the gravelly bank while trying to wrestle. The sow immediately went fishing while the cubs frolicked. She evidently called them over when she hauled her first catch to a gravelly area because they dashed through the water to her side. They nibbled at the salmon for a while but quickly returned to playing. She was still catching sockeyes when we left an hour later.

facing page |

The brown bear family meanders down a cliff to Funnel Creek. These first-summer cubs will stay with their mother through another winter and summer.

The female bear would have continued caring for her cubs through last winter and into this summer. It may be about now, in September, that she will chase them away, or maybe she will wait until the following spring. Possibly, they will be approaching her size, fat for the winter after a good summer of eating salmon, berries, and lush grass. Katmai National Park is protected in the park system and as a wilderness area. A place that provides all their needs is critical for their survival. This protection will deal with most internal threats, but the bears are still susceptible to external ones.

A bear picks a single sockeye and then pursues it with all her energy. At least seventeen others zip away from this bruin, knowing they may be next if she fails to catch her chosen quarry.

Throughout my career, I focused on protecting public lands, keeping them wild, and allowing natural ecological processes to continue functioning. The goal was to preserve an area's ecological integrity so that a native mixture of species might continue to prosper. Everglades National Park is an excellent example of the challenges of protecting native species and their ecosystems. The park encompasses over 1.5 million acres, and much of it has been brought into the National Wilderness Preservation System. Even so, the ecosystem continues to degrade, and populations of wading birds, sparrows, and other species continue to decrease. The park is downstream from a vast wetland system highly altered by humans. Development and agriculture have changed the pattern of water flow and increased the pollution levels in the park. More recently, non-native species have complicated the situation. Melaleuca, a tree from Australia, has begun to spread through the wetlands. Cichlid fish, pythons, and numerous non-native plants have invaded and changed the quality of other species' habitats. Coal-fired electricity plants along the coast have left mercury residues in rainwater. The effects of mercury poisoning have been discovered in some wading birds. Thus, even with park and wilderness designations, more threats must be addressed.

My trip to Alaska made clear to me the need for a comprehensive conservation strategy that looks well beyond the boundaries of protected areas. Wilderness designation is a crucial component of a conservation strategy, but it alone is insufficient. Four million acres protected in Katmai National Park would seem like enough land to maintain a viable population of brown bears, but the bears need sockeye salmon to reach their hibernation weights, and sockeyes need the northern Pacific Ocean for several years before returning. Warmer waters in the Pacific due to climate change and the increased acidification of the oceans from higher carbon dioxide levels are decreasing the food supplies for salmon. Consequently, the growth rates of

The mother brown bear carries a large sockeye to a gravel wash to begin feasting.

sockeyes are being reduced, and their survival may be threatened.

The gulls that migrate up the rivers to gorge on salmon scraps breed along the Pacific coast. Many of the shorebirds I searched for during my Alaska adventure move south along the coast or through the interior of North America, and some travel

as far as Tierra del Fuego. The wandering tattler and others head south, and many fly to the Pacific Islands for the winter. Shorebird species are threatened by habitat loss along their flyways and in their wintering areas. The wheatears head west to Asia, while the gray-cheeked thrushes move east and south to the Amazon. Keeping Katmai intact requires a global perspective.

We can deal with many of these problems, as seen in the recovery of the bald eagles and trumpeter swans. The banning of DDT has helped bald eagles recover, and putting a halt to market hunting has allowed trumpeter swans to rebound. It comes down to figuring out what threatens a species or an ecosystem and developing strategies to counter those problems. Preventing the construction of the Pebble Mine seems essential to maintaining Katmai, and climate change must be addressed.

On our first day in Alaska, the same female grizzly bear and her two cubs ambled along the ridge downstream from the Funnel Creek falls. They moseyed closer and closer to us. The small ones galloped along with her, not a care in the world. As she approached, I hoped she would come down to the creek where the salmon were thick and the photography would be better. She halved the distance and stood tall on her hind legs to stare at the water.

Through my binoculars, I noticed the tension in her face skyrocket, and her entire body became as stiff as a statue. The cubs continued to romp around

her, but the sow dropped to all fours, moved a few dozen yards closer, and stood again. As her body rose, the cubs became still, their eyes fixed on her. Then they bolted back down the ridge and away from us, and she took off after them at a dead run. She had seen the giant male brown bear that was hunting sockeyes less than a stone's throw away from us and decided that the future of her cubs was at risk. We need more people to think about the future of those cubs and help our society change so that they and their descendants can continue to prosper.

A fall 2020 article in the *New York Times* asks, "How will you tell the story of your response to the coronavirus in ten years?" The piece challenges people not to let their story be one of defeat but to make it one of resilience. Seattle is filled with smoke from wildfires occurring across the West on this September day, a year after my Alaska trip, adding to the sense of gloom from the COVID-19 pandemic. Climate change has resulted in hotter fires covering larger areas. Over five million acres burned in Washington, Oregon, and California in 2020. Health departments recommended that we stay inside. The smoke also affected the birds. I've seen less activity at my feeders. COVID-19 continues to restrict our movements, and masks are required in places where we can go. It's hard to think about things other than our health.

facing page |

A brown bear family fishes for sockeye salmon along Funnel Creek. The mother calls the cubs over to eat while she goes back to fishing. Gulls lurk all around, waiting for leftovers.

A few birds flit around my patio, even in the smoke, continuing their lives. Maybe Alaska has taught me that I should continue studying how the earth works and then help people see those things about nature, birds, and geology that excite me—try to cultivate in them that sense of awe and wonder that stirs my blood. We need more people to care about the world if we are to protect nature at all levels. The author of the *Times* article suggests that we look to the future and not dwell on the past.

The image of the caribou's long legs comes to mind. Their graceful movements mesmerize me; they show no inhibition or restraint. During the pandemic, I can't go to distant lands as planned to see birds and wildlife and study the science that has fascinated me all my life. But there's much to see and learn in Washington and the Pacific Northwest. Perhaps the coronavirus and the wildfires suggest a different focus for me—one that helps connect people to the wild and its wonders so strongly that they will care enough to take action. Maybe the caribou and bears I was able to see in Alaska will inspire me with the perseverance I need to pursue these new possibilities and reshape my life.

On this September day in Seattle, the black-headed grosbeak hops into the bush above the feeder, wiping her bill a few times on a branch before dashing into the next yard. Maybe that unsettled mood on my first morning in Alaska was my subconscious flirting with me. It knew that Alaska was more than a chance to photograph bears. It would be a gift that might help me move entirely into a new, post-career life, one that could handle disruptions like the COVID-19 pandemic and remain focused on the future.

To be sure, the change in me has been incremental over the last few years: a new house, new friends, and new passions. However, nature has been an integral part of my life's journey. My mother gave me the gift of loving nature, and perhaps my career was an attempt to give something back to nature, an effort to protect it and restore its integrity. Over the previous seven years, nature has lavished me with gifts, helping me erect a ladder out of despair and then build a new life. Even during the COVID-19 pandemic, it permeates my home, my daily routine, always offering something.

Two juncos replace the grosbeak on the feeder. As Lewis Hyde writes in *The Gift: How the Creative Spirit Transforms the World*, passing that item along is the act of gratitude that finishes the labor. Nature has always given me a gift, but the isolation I experienced during the COVID-19 pandemic gave me space to reflect on Alaska, realize its gift, and complete my transformation. The brown bears, the caribou, and wildlands have my gratitude for helping fuel the final metamorphosis of my soul. I'm ready to pass it along.

| A dark-eyed junco sits on the fence in my Seattle yard, waiting for its turn at the bird feeder.

AFTERWORD

The threat of the Pebble Mine construction loomed over my time in Alaska and while I wrote this book. Much has happened since 2020, and a review will help put this issue in perspective.

The mineral deposits north of Lake Iliamna were discovered in the 1980s. The Northern Dynasty Minerals Corporation acquired the mineral rights in early 2001 and began the permitting process. The company sponsored extensive surveys of the area to determine the ore quantity and to evaluate the possible environmental consequences. In 2010, the EPA took the lead in assessing the potential mine by launching the Bristol Bay Watershed Assessment.

In July 2012, "Alaska Gold," which aired on PBS's *Frontline*, gave a good overview of the environmental resources at stake and the gold, copper, molybdenum, and other minerals available for exploitation. In 2023, they made this episode available through various outlets, providing an excellent background to this controversy. Former Alaska State Senator Rick Halford, who opposed the mine, said in that documentary, "I believe this will be the biggest environmental fight of this century for Alaska."

In 2014, the EPA ruled that the mine would cause irreparable damage to the environment and negatively affect the livelihoods of Native people in the region. Their report stated, "The mining of the Pebble deposit at any of these sizes, even the smallest, could result in significant and unacceptable adverse effects on ecologically important streams, wetlands, lakes, and ponds and the fishery areas they support." The EPA denied the permit, and the company immediately appealed the ruling. The appeal process was underway when the Trump administration took over. They settled the appeal, allowing a new permit application to be submitted. They also turned the permitting process over to the Army Corps of Engineers and removed it from the EPA's jurisdiction. In 2019, when I was in Alaska, the Corps was analyzing the environmental effects this project might cause.

In July 2020, the Army Corps released its environmental impact statement. The impact statement was not the permit but rather the analysis of the possible mine's damage to the environment. Their study concluded that the permit should not be issued until more research and better plans had been put together. Senator Murkowski released a statement saying, "After this very rigorous, very thorough process, the [Army Corps of Engineers] has found that the Pebble project as currently proposed does not meet that high bar. And I have said, if you don't meet the high bar, then a permit should not be issued."

In July 2020, Donald Trump Jr. tweeted that the mine shouldn't be built even though the presi-

facing page |

A brown bear chases a sockeye through the shallows. Protecting the ecological integrity of Katmai National Park and Preserve will require a comprehensive conservation strategy that looks well beyond the borders of this crown jewel.

dent—his father—continued to support the mine. By fall 2020, President Trump had dropped his support for the mine.

In November 2021, the EPA reinitiated a Clean Water Act review and, in May 2022, released recommendations for stronger protections in the headwaters of Bristol Bay. In January 2023, the Army Corps of Engineers denied the permit applications. A few days later, the EPA, citing its authority under the Clean Water Act, issued a "final determination" that the proposed mine would have "unacceptable adverse effects." The EPA said, "The Bristol Bay watershed is a vital economic driver, providing jobs, sustenance, and significant ecological and cultural value to the region."

Alaska's governor, Mike Dunleavy, and many other state politicians decried the ruling, claiming it usurps the state's "ability and responsibility to protect its own fishery resources." Governor Dunleavy stated, "Alarmingly, it lays the foundation to stop any development project, mining or non-mining, in any area of Alaska with wetlands and fish-bearing streams. My administration will stand up for the rights of Alaskans, Alaska property owners, and Alaska's future." The mining company also said this decision was "not supported legally, technically, or environmentally."

The EPA used its "veto authority" under Section 404c of the Clean Water Act to stop the mine. This veto is only the fourteenth time a federal agency has used this authority in fifty years, and these rulings have always stood in the courts. One might think this mine project is now dead, but in summer 2023, in a separate case, the Supreme Court ruled that the EPA could not prevent a couple from building a house on a wetland adjacent to an Idaho lake. Effectively, they restricted the scope of the Clean Water Act that had been in place for fifty years. The Idaho decision doesn't speak well of what might happen if the mine developers and the state government take their case to the Supreme Court or if a new administration takes a different view of the matter.

The fight to protect Bristol Bay will continue.

facing page |

A glaucous-winged gull snatches a salmon scrap from a brown bear, who then puts on a chase. The interaction illustrates the complex food web: prey, predator, and scavenger. The ocean nutrients that the salmon bring back to Alaska help support the ecosystem.

ACKNOWLEDGMENTS

Bob Harvey organized this trip to the Katmai Peninsula, planning an excellent itinerary. He kindly allowed me to join his group, Nature Photography Adventures, and then looked after me as I trudged across the tundra. His humor, kindness, and knowledge contributed significantly to the joy of my being there.

Our pilots and guides—Glen Alsworth Sr., Glen Alsworth Jr., Leo Fowler, and Carlon Voran—flew us safely and expertly across the Katmai, sharing their knowledge of this beautiful country. Because of them, I learned a tremendous amount about the spectacular Alaska wilderness. Seeing a place through the eyes of someone who loves it is an honor and privilege I cherish.

My colleagues in our Everglades work helped me develop my views on science, conservation, restoration, and large landscapes. I would like to acknowledge Wayne Hoffman, Allan Strong, and Reed Bowman, who each led different parts of our research. I especially thank Tom Martin. Tom came to Florida to lead Audubon's Everglades policy initiative and introduced me to the ins and outs of making change happen. He opened doors, pushed me through, and helped me see a new direction for my career.

I can't thank Bill Meadows enough. He hired me to be part of his senior team at The Wilderness Society and then stood beside me, mentoring me as I attempted to tackle the science-policy interface. I thank all the staff of the Research Department for their knowledge and feedback, as well as the staffs of the other departments at The Wilderness Society. I especially acknowledge Jerry Greenberg, Pete Morton, Greg Aplet, and Mike Anderson, who played pivotal roles in my work.

Although my second time at National Audubon was too short, I learned a lot and was able to focus on bird conservation once again. My interactions with regional conservation, policy, and communications staff benefited me greatly. I especially want to acknowledge Glenn Olson, Stan Senner, Greg Butcher, and John Cecil. My opportunity to work with BirdLife International and partner organizations across the globe helped me think about conservation on another scale.

My good friend Danielle Graham kindly read an early draft of this manuscript and gave me insights into what was working and what wasn't. Two anonymous reviewers provided valuable suggestions that made the text more robust and the overall focus more powerful.

I can't come close to articulating how much I have learned about writing and developing essays under Christine Hemp's guidance. She has mentored my journey in this writing endeavor, coaching, encouraging, and pushing me. No words can express my gratitude and how fortunate I feel to have been able to partner with her.

facing page |

Glaciers carve the valleys in the Alaskan Range, revealing the geological processes that have shaped our earth. Plate tectonics continue to build these mountains, and snow, ice, and weather erode the rocks. Life flourishes where it can.

I thank Linda C. Bathgate, Caryn Lee Lawton, Melissa Smith, Tracy Randall, and Kerry S. Darnall of Washington State University Press for their advice and guidance on this project. Christina Dubois helped polish the final manuscript. Her insights into writing helped organize my thoughts and greatly improved the manuscript. Patrick Brommer designed a beautiful cover. They and all the staff at the Press have helped me enter the world of book publishing. I appreciate their enthusiasm for this project.

My mother, Barbara Byers Bancroft, cultivated my love of nature. My sister Barbie helped it blossom. Mother taught me the importance of naming things and encouraged my pursuit of birds. Barbie took me on long walks and horseback rides. She taught me to catch minnows, salamanders, and crawfish, and impressed on me the importance of protecting the environment. I thank them both.

I thank my daughter Kelsie for all her love and all the help she has provided; through her eyes, I have learned to look at life and this planet in new ways. And finally, my late wife Ann, who was integral to my life's journey, standing by me as I pursued birds and nature, supporting me and moving with me to jobs across the country—I miss you.

A creek meanders down a valley north of Lake Clark, forming extensive wetlands home to moose, beaver, birds, and waterfowl. Sockeyes spawn in the tributaries of Lake Clark and fry live in the wetlands for a year or more before heading to the sea. Boreal forests cover the uplands in these mountains.

BIBLIOGRAPHY

#Bring Birds Back. "3 Billion Birds Gone." https://www.3billionbirds.org.

Bacon, C. R., A. J. Bennett, N. Bennington, E. E. Berg, M. Brooks, H. A. Coletti, M. L. Coombs, et al. "Volcanoes of Katmai and the Alaska Peninsula." *Alaska Park Science* 11, no. 1 (2012). https://irma.nps.gov/DataStore/DownloadFile/522754.

Blom, Philipp. *Nature's Mutiny: How the Little Ice Age of the Long Seventeenth Century Transformed the West and Shaped the Present.* New York: Liveright Publishing Corporation, a division of W. W. Norton & Co., 2019.

Brna, P. J., and L. A. Verbrugge (eds). *Wildlife Resources of the Nushagak and Kvichak River Watersheds, Alaska. Final Report.* Anchorage: Anchorage Fish and Wildlife Field Office, U.S. Fish and Wildlife Service, 2013.

Environmental Defense Fund. "How Will Climate Change Affect Alaska?" https://www.edf.org/sites/default/files/content/regional_releases_alaska_web_version.pdf.

EPA (U.S. Environmental Protection Agency). *An Assessment of Potential Mining Impacts on Salmon Ecosystems of Bristol Bay, Alaska, Vol. 1—Main Report.* EPA 910-R-14-001. Seattle: Region 10, 2014. https://www.epa.gov/sites/default/files/2015-05/documents/bristol_bay_assessment_final_2014_vol1.pdf.

———. *Proposed Determination of U.S. Environmental Protection Agency Region 10 Pursuant to Section 404(c) of the Clean Water Act, Pebble Deposit Area, Southwest Alaska.* Seattle: Region 10, 2014. https://www.epa.gov/bristolbay/2014-proposed-determination-pursuant-section-404c-clean-water-act-pebble-deposit-area.

Fitz, Michael. *The Bears of Brooks Falls: Wildlife and Survival on Alaska's Brooks River.* New York: Countryman Press, a division of W. W. Norton & Co., 2021.

Fitzpatrick, John W., and Peter P. Marra. "The Crisis for Birds Is a Crisis for Us All." *New York Times*, 19 September 2019, Opinion. https://www.nytimes.com/2019/09/19/opinion/crisis-birds-north-america.html.

facing page and detail right |

Three sockeye salmon twist together in the shallows. Two males might be vying for a single female. Sockeyes spawn in the shallows, where the fertilized eggs settle among the gravel.

Fjeldså, J., L. Christidis, and P. G. P. Ericson (eds.). *The Largest Avian Radiation: The Evolution of Perching Birds, or the Order Passeriformes.* Barcelona: Lynx Nature Books, 2020.

Florida Natural Areas Inventory. https://www.fnai.org.

Frontline. Season 2012, episode 16, "Alaska Gold." Aired July 23, 2012, on PBS. https://www.pbs.org/video/frontline-alaska-gld/.

Gaglioti, B. V., D. H. Mann, G. C. Wiles, B. M. Jones, J. Charlton, N. Wiesenberg, and L. Andreu-Hayles. "Timing and Potential Causes of 19th-Century Glacier Advances in Coastal Alaska Based on Tree-Ring Dating and Historical Accounts." *Frontiers in Earth Science* 7 (2019). https://doi.org/10.3389/feart.2019.00082.

Hickey, H. "Mountain glaciers shrinking across the West." *UW News*, 20 October 2017. https://www.washington.edu/news/2017/10/20/mountain-glaciers-shrinking-across-the-west/.

Hildreth, Wes, and Judy Fierstein. *The Novarupta-Katmai Eruption of 1912—Largest Eruption of the Twentieth Century: Centennial Perspective.* U.S. Geological Survey Professional Paper 1791. Reston, VA: USGS, 2012. https://pubs.usgs.gov/pp/1791/pp1791.pdf.

Holden, Emily. "Climate Change Is Having Widespread Health Impacts." *Scientific American*, 16 September 2019. https://www.scientificamerican.com/article/climate-change-is-having-widespread-health-impacts/.

Hyde, Lewis. *The Gift: How the Creative Spirit Transforms the World*, 3rd ed. New York: Vintage Books, 2019.

Kimmerer, Robin W. *Braiding Sweetgrass: Indigenous Wisdom, Scientific Knowledge, and the Teachings of Plants*, illust. ed. Minneapolis: Milkweed Editions, 2020.

———. *Gathering Moss: A Natural and Cultural History of Mosses.* Corvallis: Oregon State University Press, 2003.

McKibben, Bill. "Money Is the Oxygen on Which the Fire of Global Warming Burns." *The New Yorker*, 17 September 2019. https://www.newyorker.com/news/daily-comment/money-is-the-oxygen-on-which-the-fire-of-global-warming-burns.

Moritsch, Barbara. "Katmai National Park and Preserve Vs. The Pebble Mine." *National Parks Traveler*, 19 January 2020. https://www.nationalparkstraveler.org/2020/01/katmai-national-park-and-preserve-vs-pebble-mine.

National Audubon Society. "Important Bird Areas." https://www.audubon.org/important-bird-areas.

National Park Service. *Bears of Brooks River 2019: A Guide to Their Identification, Lives, and Habits*. Katmai National Park and Preserve, NPS, US Department of the Interior. http://npshistory.com/publications/katm/brooks-river-bears/2019.pdf.

———. "Katmai National Park and Preserve Foundation Statement." NPS, US Department of the Interior, 2009. https://www.nps.gov/katm/learn/management/upload/KATM_Foundation_Statement_December2009-3.pdf.

———. "Lake Clark National Park and Preserve Foundation Statement." NPS, US Department of the Interior, 2009. https://parkplanning.nps.gov/document.cfm?documentID=26497.

North American Nature Photography Association. "Principles of Ethical Field Practices." https://nanpa.org/wp-content/uploads/sites/48/Files/Public/Ethical-Field-Practices-Revised-3-2018.pdf.

Olson, Sigurd F. *Reflections from the North Country*. New York: Knopf, 1976.

Oreskes, N., M. Oppenheimer, and D. Jameson. "Scientists Have Been Underestimating the Pace of Climate Change." *Scientific American*, 19 August 2019. https://www.scientificamerican.com/blog/observations/scientists-have-been-underestimating-the-pace-of-climate-change/.

Proenneke, Richard, and Sam Keith. *One Man's Wilderness: An Alaskan Odyssey*. Anchorage: Alaska Northwest Books, 1999.

Santer, Ben. "Rock Climbing, Climate Science and Leadership." *Scientific American*, 16 September 2019. https://www.scientificamerican.com/article/rock-climbing-climate-science-and-leadership/.

Sarton, May, The Journals of. *Journal of a Solitude*. London: Women's Press, 1985.

Stanford Environmental Law Society. *The Endangered Species Act*. Stanford, CA: Stanford University Press, 2001.

Suring, Lowell. *Brown Bears and the Pebble Project in Southwest Alaska*. Technical Bulletin 2020-1. Northern Ecologic L.L.C., 2020. http://dx.doi.org/10.13140/RG.2.2.31574.57923.

The Wilderness Society. "Alaska: America's Last Wild Frontier." https://www.wilderness.org/wild-places/alaska.

United States Congress. *The Clean Water Act as Amended by the Water Quality Act of 1987, Public Law 100-4.* Washington, DC: USGPO, 1988.

Whitaker, D. M., I. G. Warkentin, J. P. B. McDermott, P. E. Lowther, C. C. Rimmer, B. Kessel, S. L. Johnson, et al. "Gray-cheeked Thrush (*Catharus minimus*)," version 1.0. In *Birds of the World* (P. G. Rodewald, ed.). Ithaca, NY: Cornell Lab of Ornithology, 2020. Last updated 17 May 2018. https://doi.org/10.2173/bow.gycthr.01.

Western Hemisphere Shorebird Reserve Network. "Conserving Shorebirds and their habitat through a network of key sites across the Americas." https://whsrn.org.

Williams, Florence. *The Nature Fix: Why Nature Makes Us Happier, Healthier, and More Creative.* New York: W. W. Norton & Co., 2017.

Woody, Carol Ann, and Sarah L. O'Neal. *Effects of Copper on Fish and Aquatic Resources.* Anchorage: Fisheries Research and Consulting and The Nature Conservancy, 2012. https://www.conservationgateway.org/ConservationByGeography/NorthAmerica/UnitedStates/alaska/sw/cpa/Documents/W2013ECopperF062012.pdf.

Young, M. A., and C. S. Adkisson. "Pine Grosbeak (*Pinicola enucleator*)," version 2.0. In *Birds of the World* (P. G. Rodewald, B. K. Keeney, and S. M. Billerman, eds.). Ithaca, NY: Cornell Lab of Ornithology, 2020. https://doi.org/10.2173/bow.pingro.02.

INDEX

Numbers in italics indicate illustrations

facing page |

A brown bear stares back toward where I stood and pauses briefly before heading into Funnel Creek.

ABOUT THE AUTHOR

Thomas Bancroft's lifelong passion for birds and nature has been the driving force behind his illustrious career. His earliest memory is of his mother helping him identify black-capped chickadees. He was five. Growing up on a farm, he was constantly immersed in the beauty of nature. This love for the natural world led him to pursue these interests in undergraduate and graduate school. Thomas holds a Ph.D. in Biology and an M.A. in Zoology, both from the University of South Florida. He led a research program on Everglades conservation for over a decade, during which time he helped craft restoration and management plans for this spectacular wild area.

A move to Washington, DC, put Thomas at the nexus of science and policy, where he was Vice President of the Research Department at The Wilderness Society and then Chief Scientist at the National Audubon Society. He focused on synthesizing science to influence policy and management plans. For The Wilderness Society, Thomas was pivotal in building integrated conservation programs across the West and Alaska, encompassing science, policy, advocacy, and communication.

Achieving conservation goals requires people to care. Policies and laws reflect our values, which come from caring. Since moving to Seattle, Thomas has focused on sharing his love and passion for nature, helping others see details in nature that they may otherwise miss. He teaches, makes presentations, leads hikes, and writes. His articles and photographs have appeared in numerous publications. Thomas received the 2020 Mountaineers Service Award for his outreach to the broader community in Washington State.

The author searches for birds at Portage Lake in Lake Clark National Park and Preserve.

Two harlequin ducks fly along Funnel Creek. These birds eat aquatic insects. Salmon carcasses help fertilize the food chain by bringing ocean nutrients to these waters.